I
AM A
NUMB3R

RIAN HUGHE2

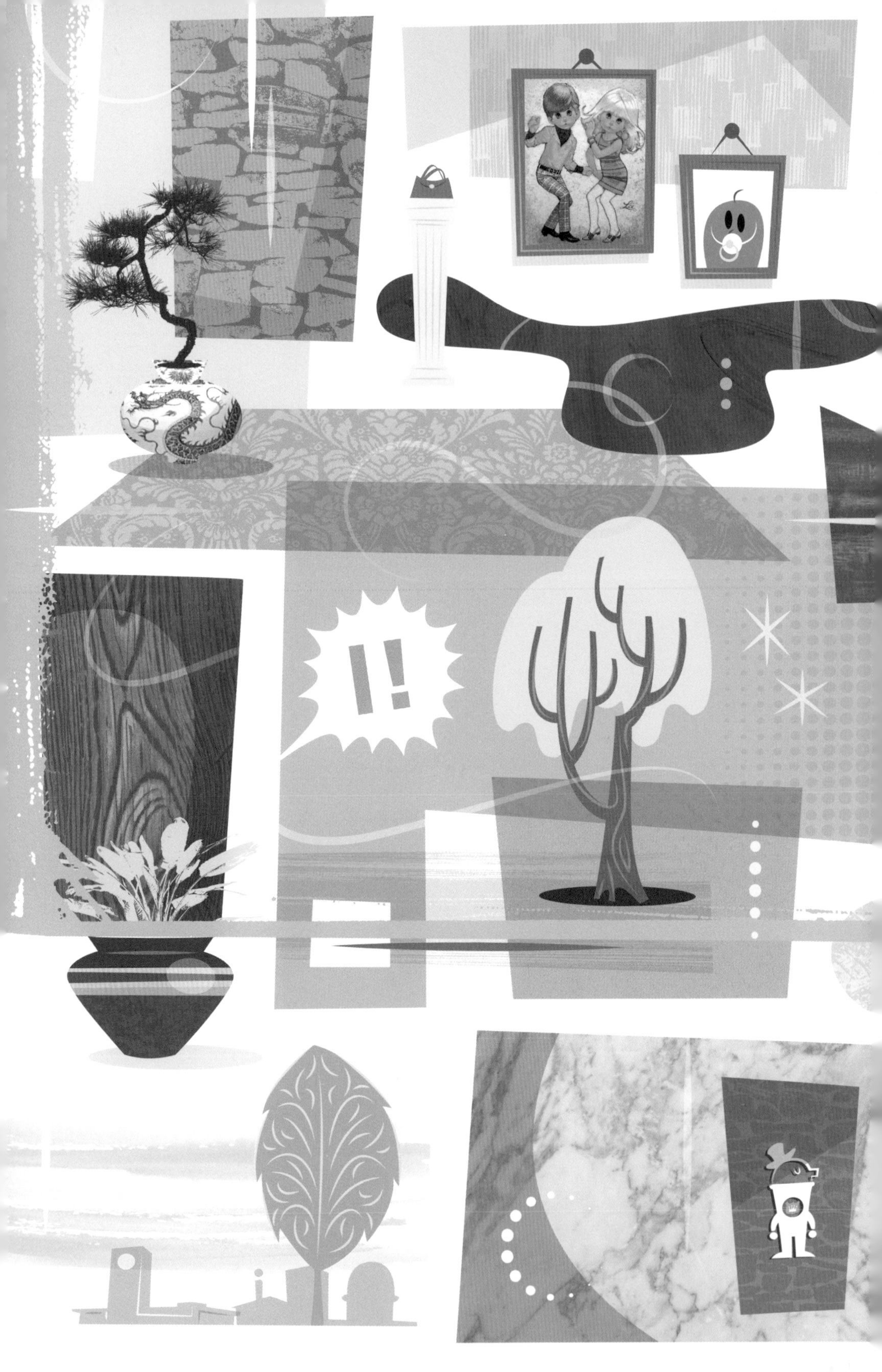
!!

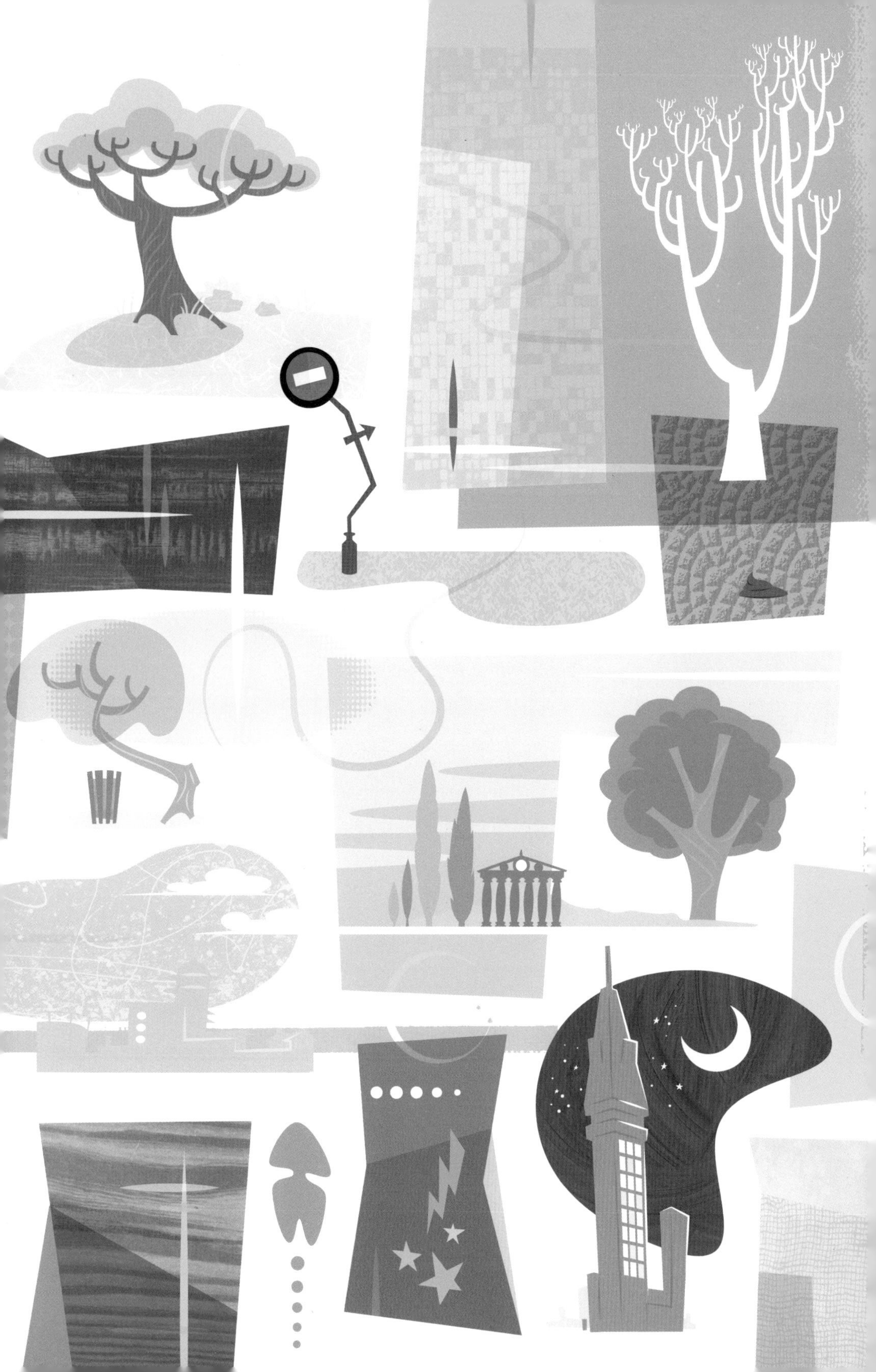

I Am A Number © 2017 Rian Hughes

Published by
Top Shelf Productions
PO Box 1282
Marietta, GA 30061-1282
USA

Editor-in-Chief: Chris Staros

Top Shelf Productions is an imprint of IDW Publishing,
a division of Idea and Design Works, LLC.
Offices: 2765 Truxtun Road
San Diego, CA 92106
USA

Visit our online catalog at
www.topshelfcomix.com

www.rianhughes.com

Printed in Korea

ISBN 978-1-60309-419-1

2021 2020 2019 2018 2017 10 9 8 7 6 5 4 3 2 1

1 AM A NUMBER

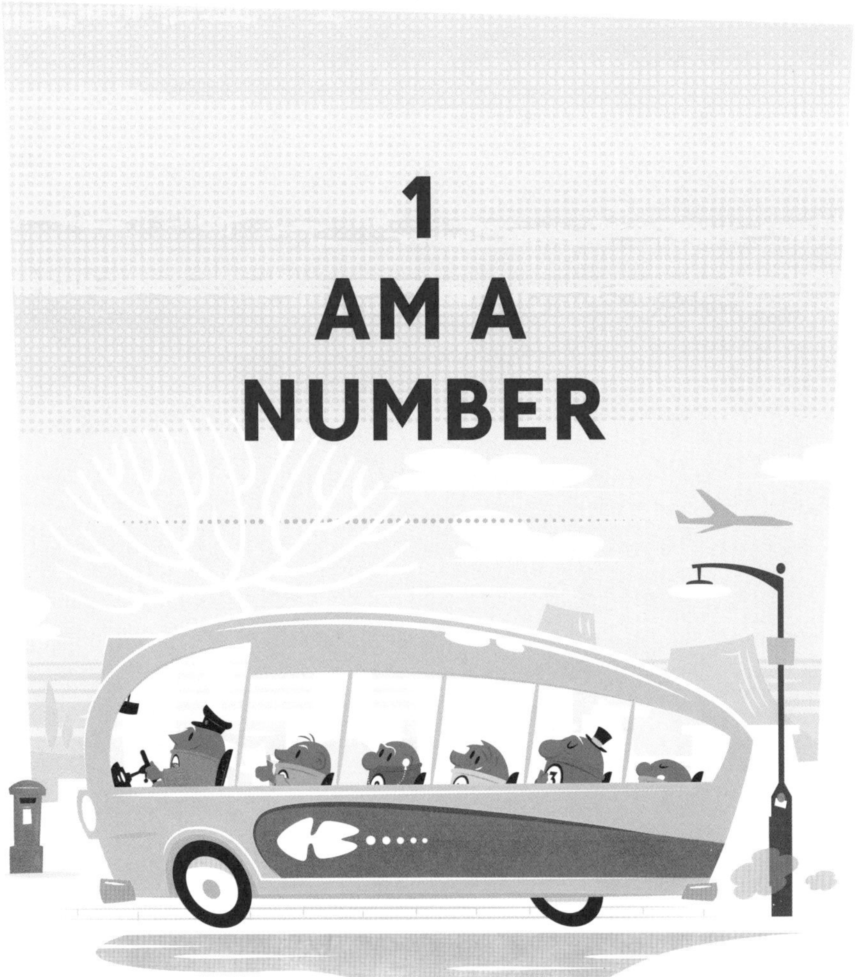

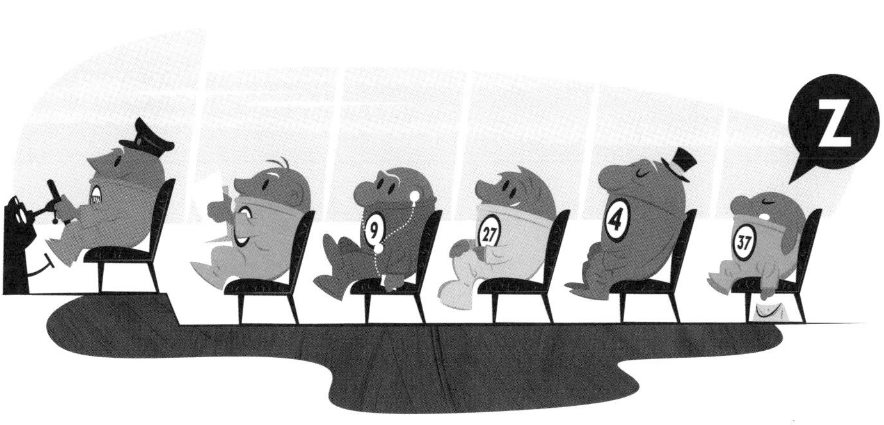
Z
9
27
4
37

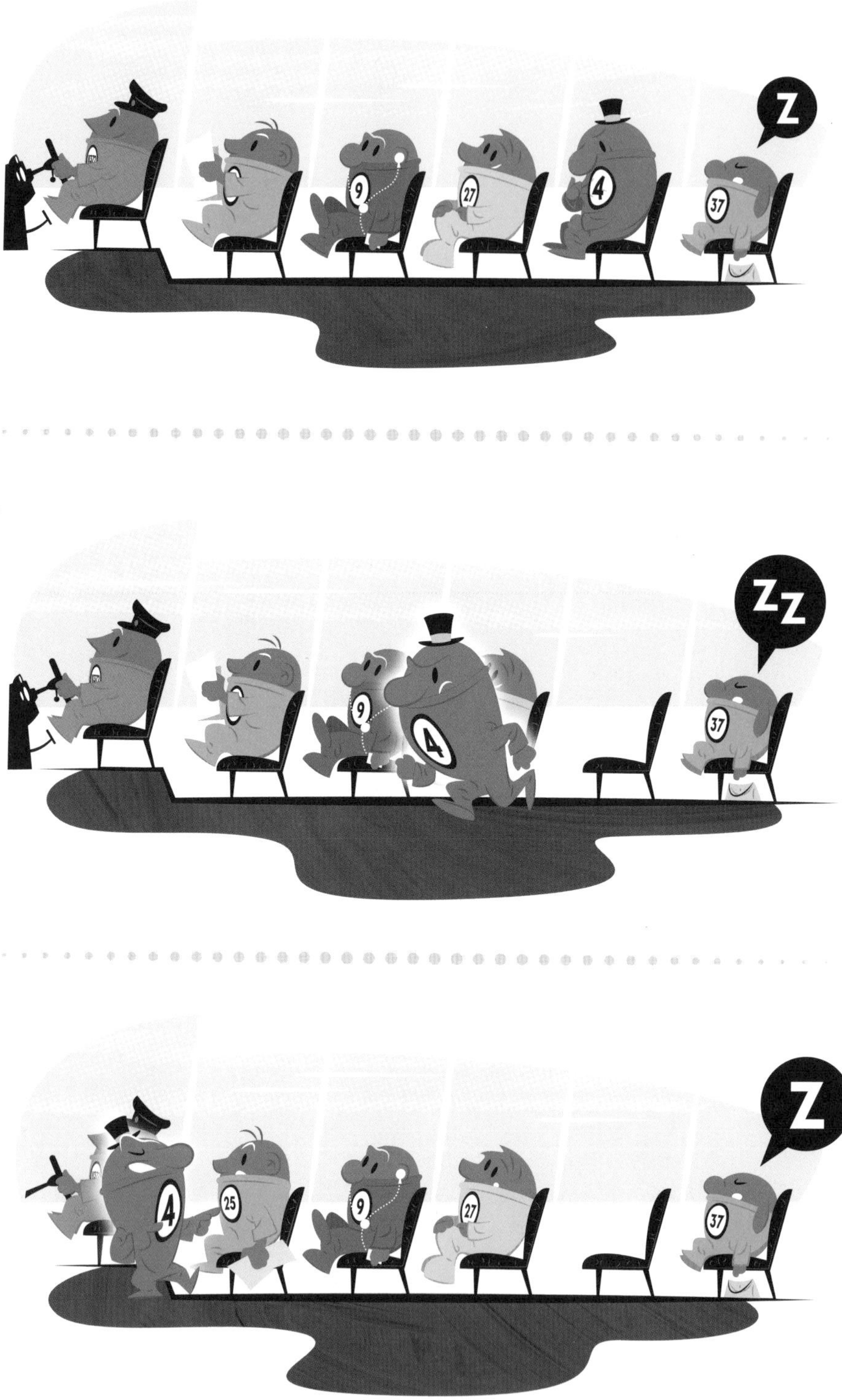
Z
ZZ
Z

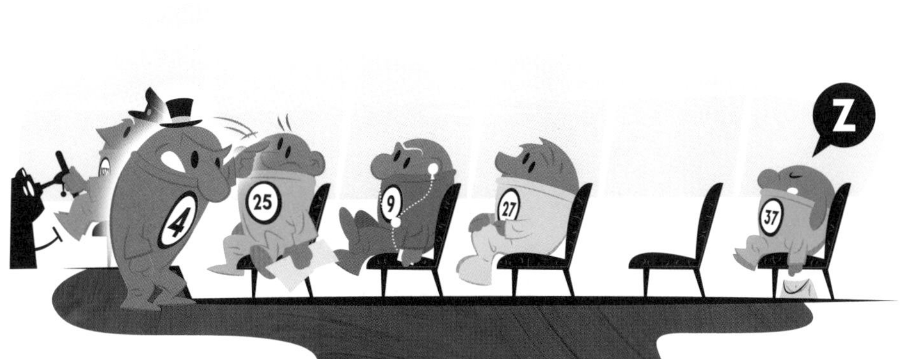
Z

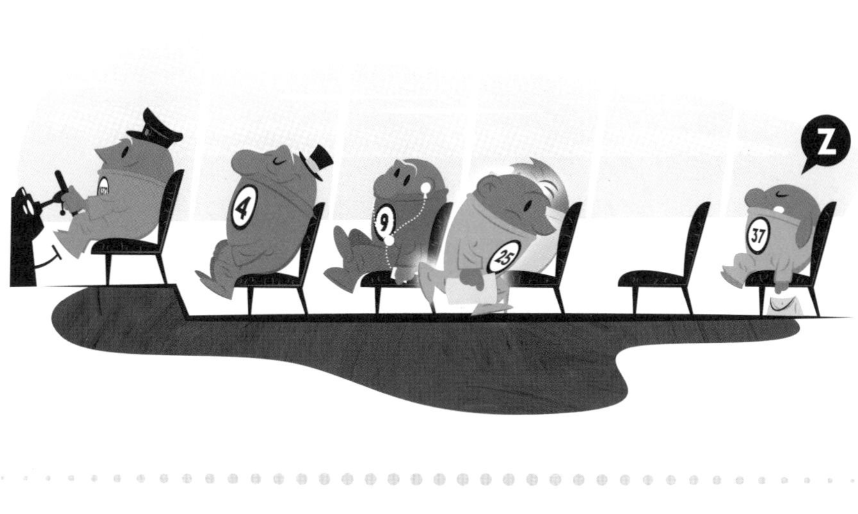
Z

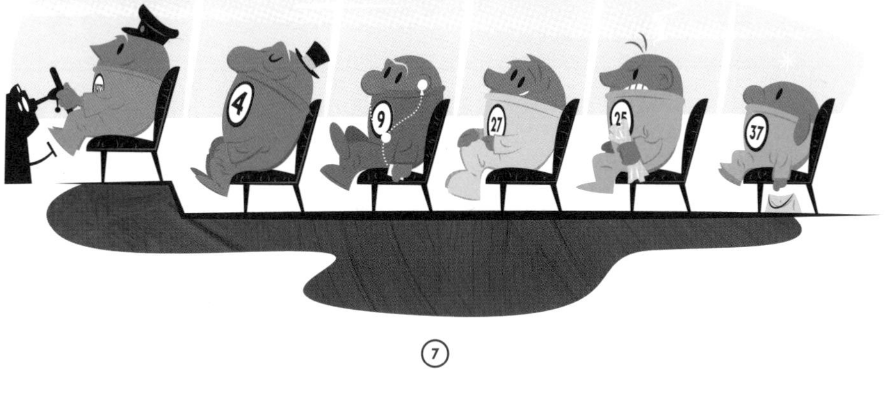

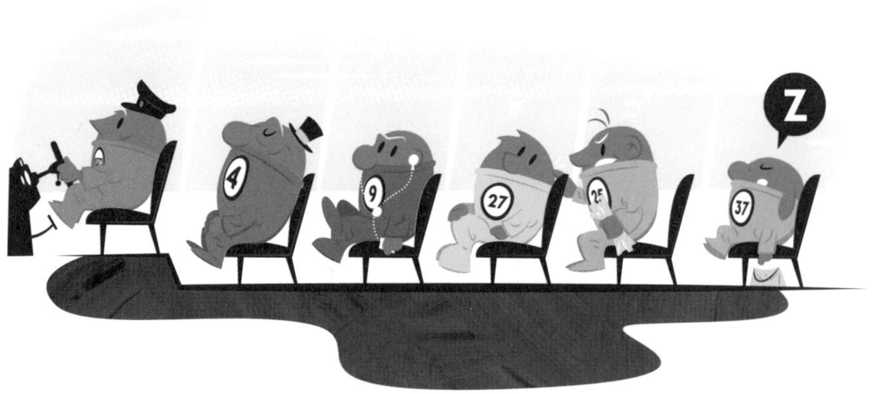
4
9
27
25
37
Z

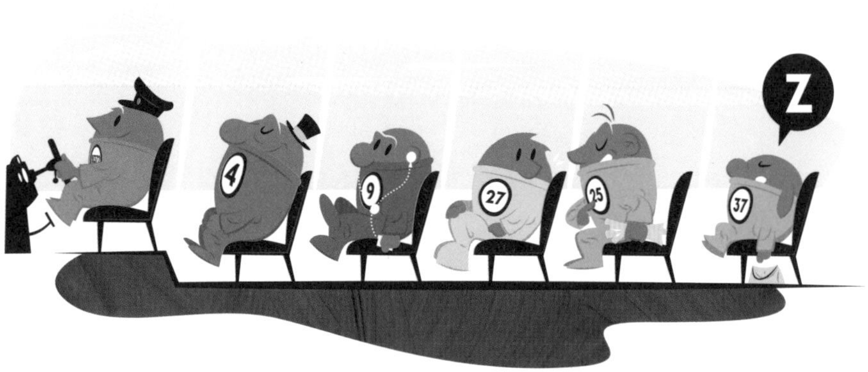
4
9
27
25
37
Z

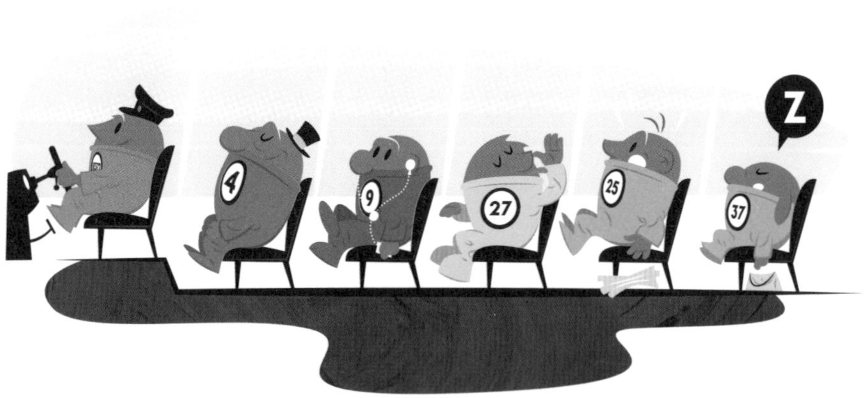
4
9
27
25
37
Z

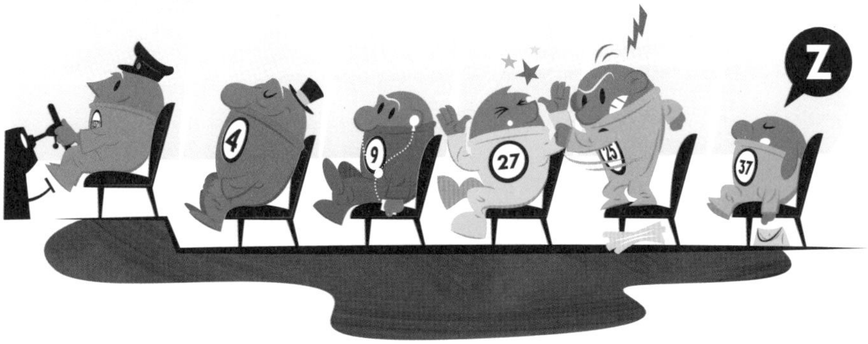

Z

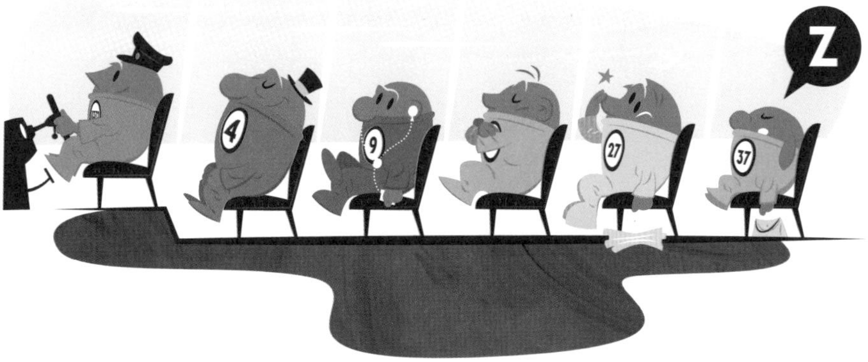

Z

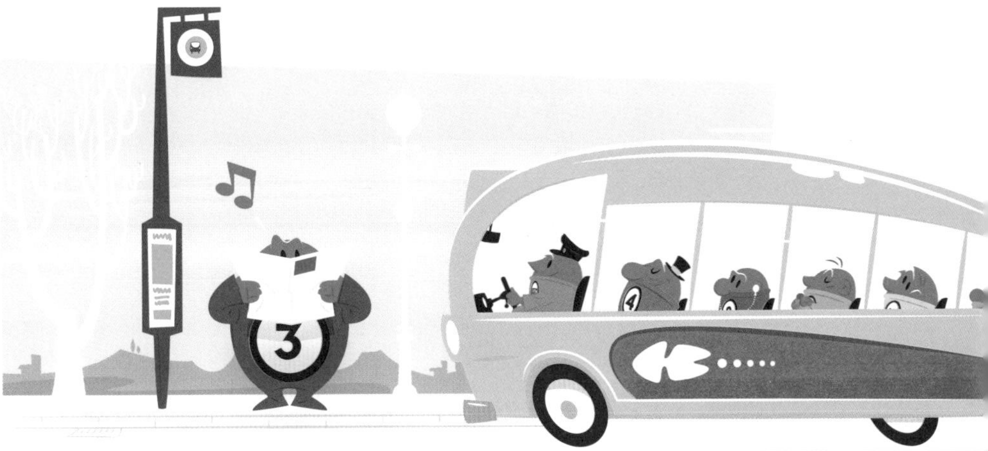

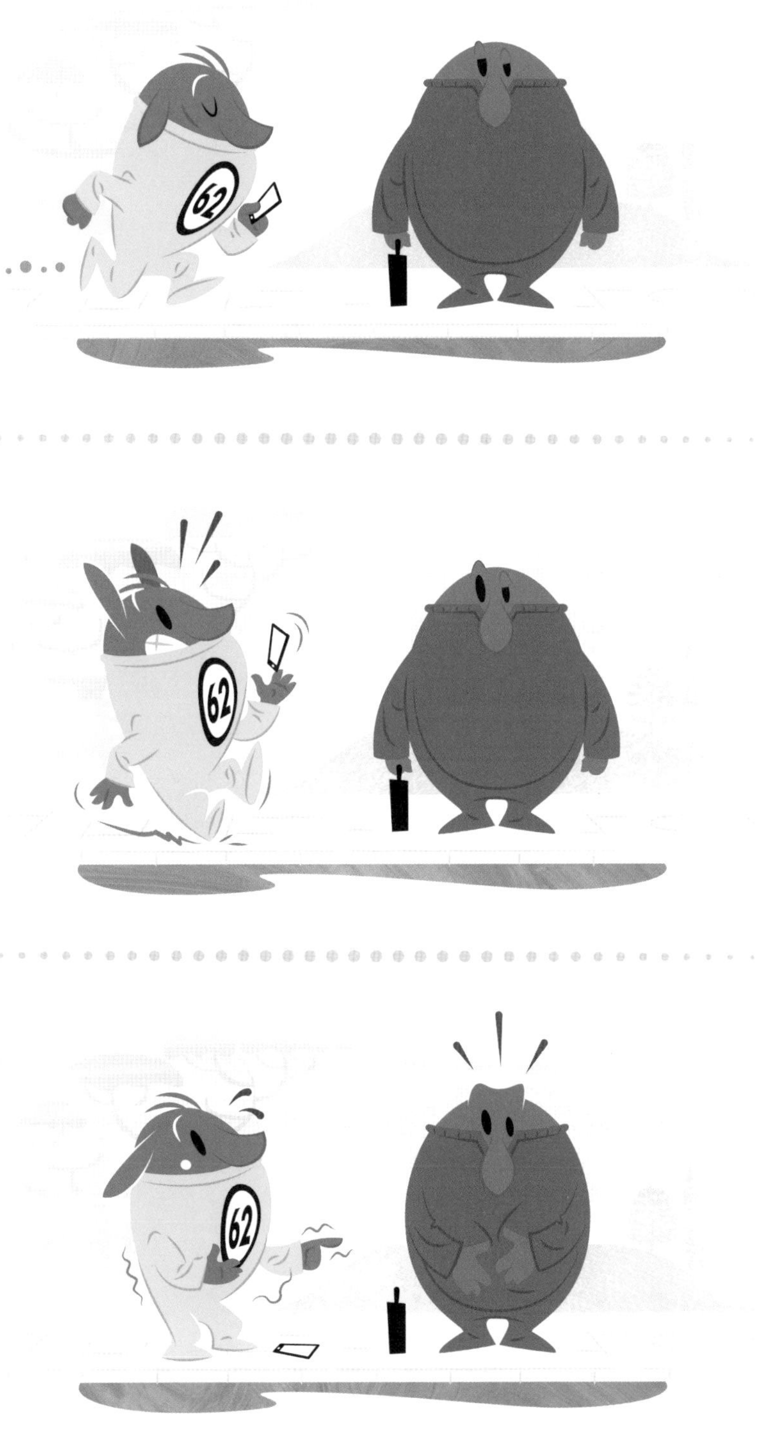
62
62
62

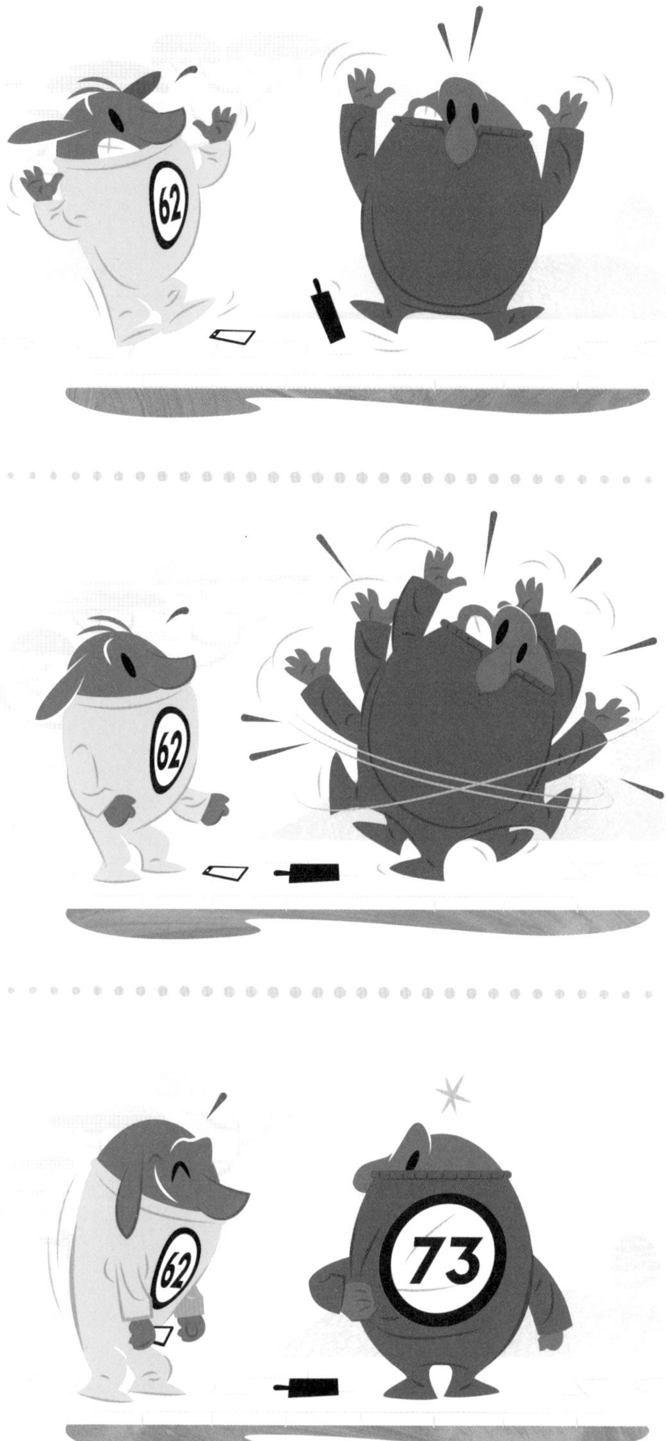
62
62
62
73

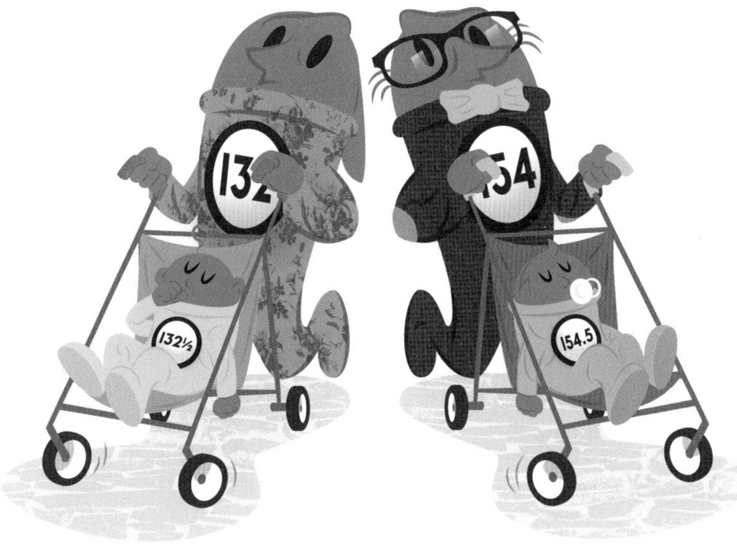
132
132½
154
154.5

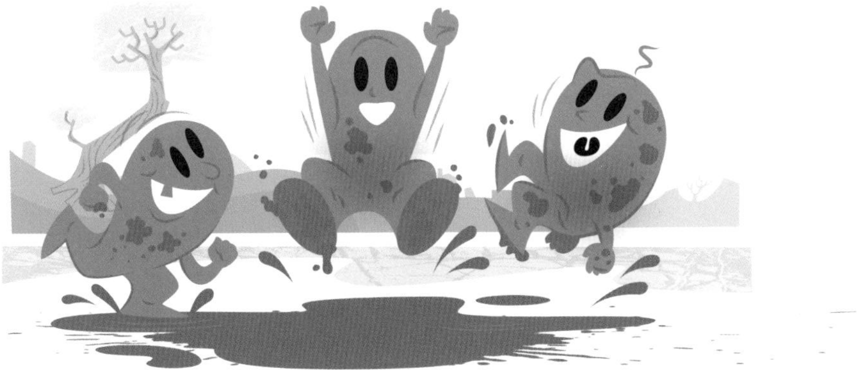

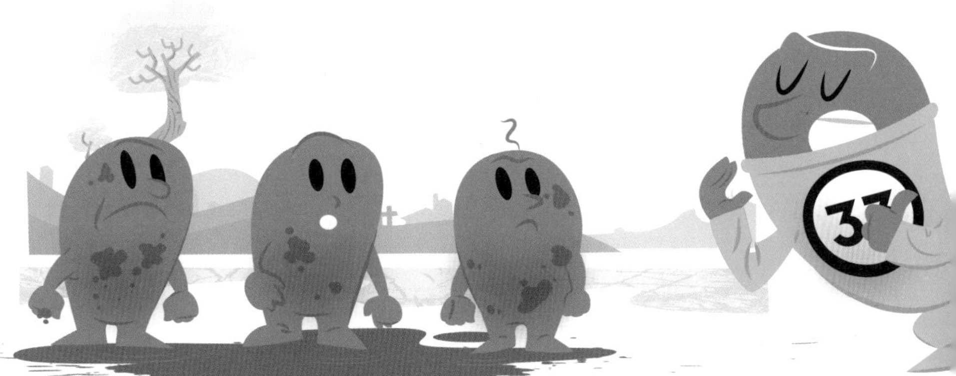
33

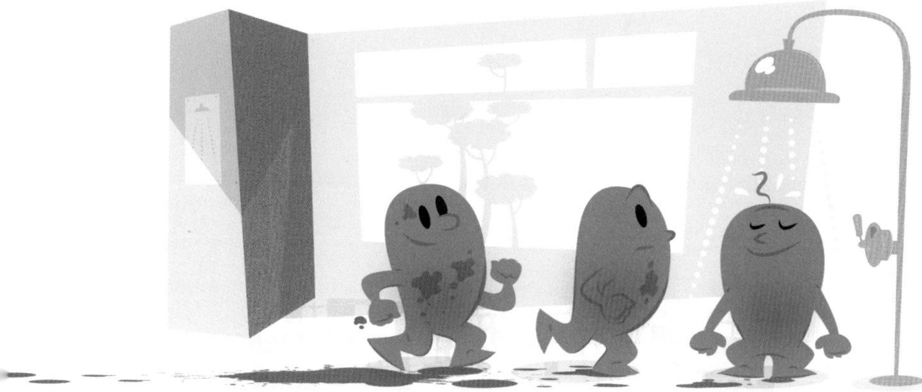

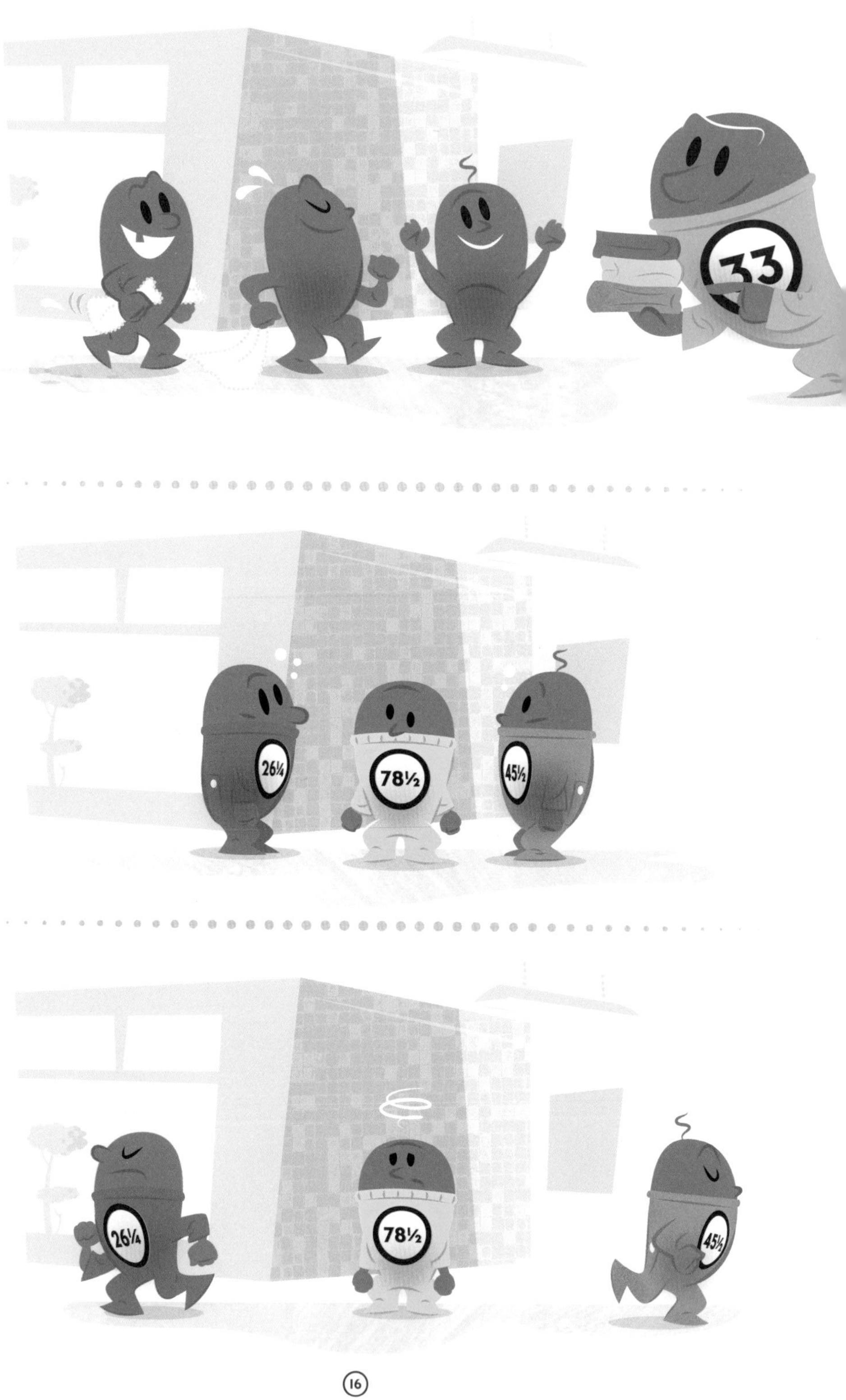
33
26¼
78½
45½
26¼
78½
45½

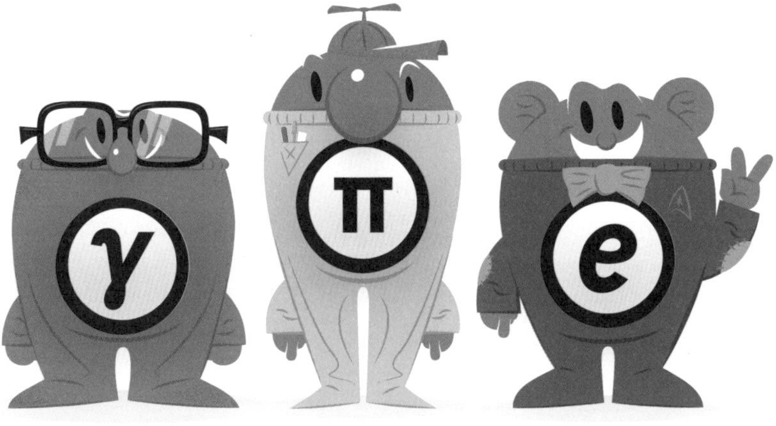
γ
π
e

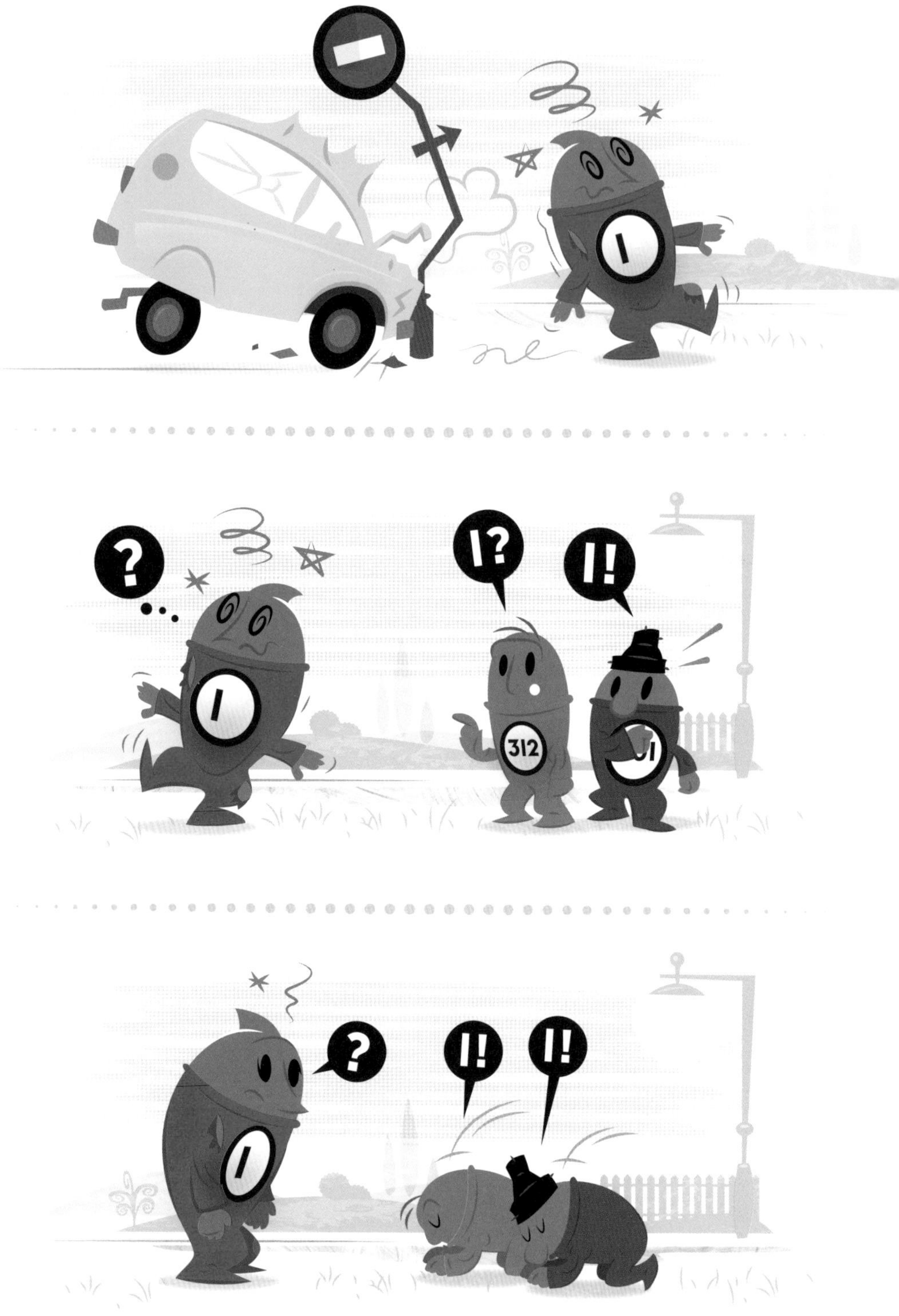
?
1?
1!
?
1!
1!

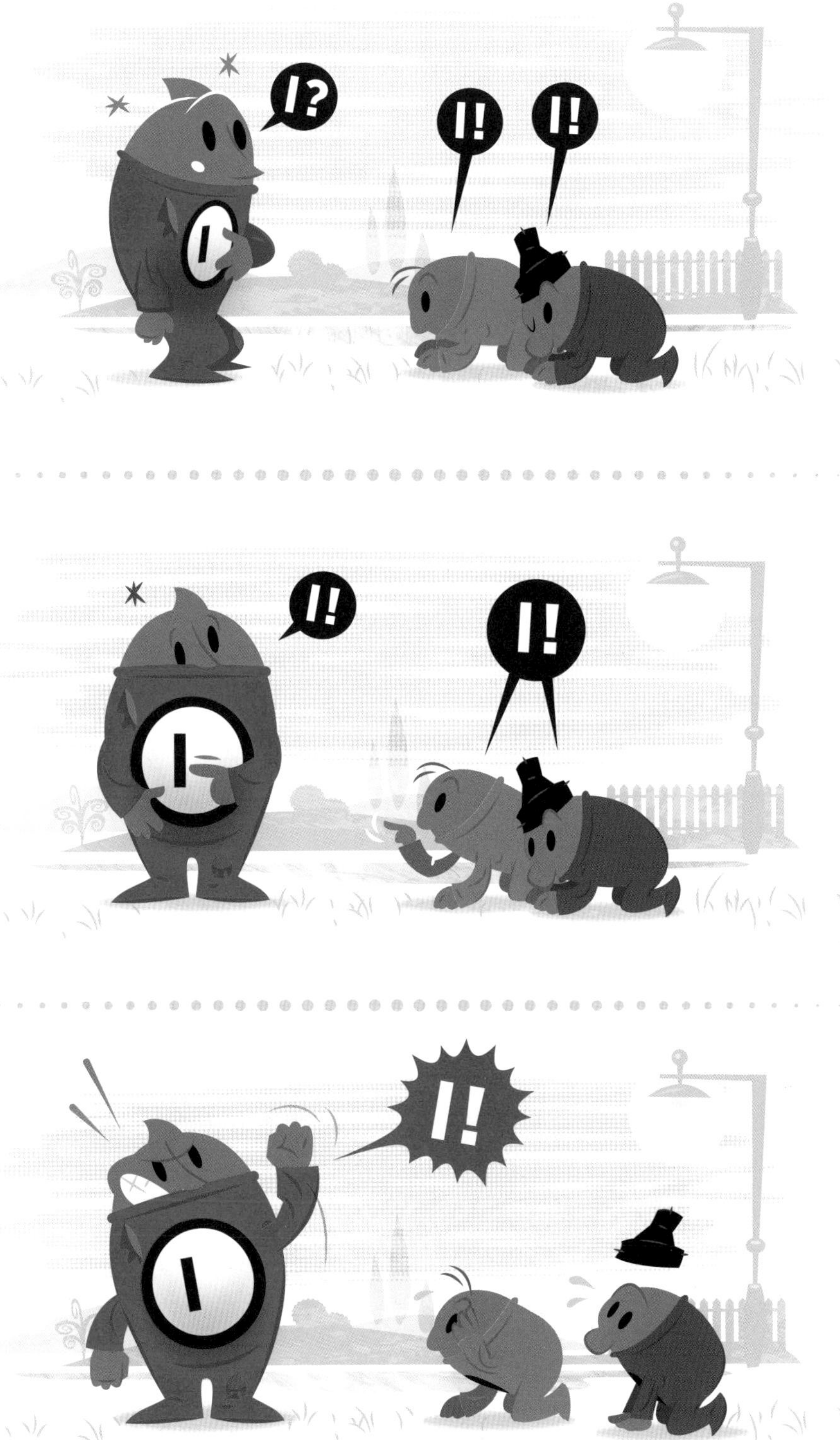
I?
I!
I!
I!
I!
I!

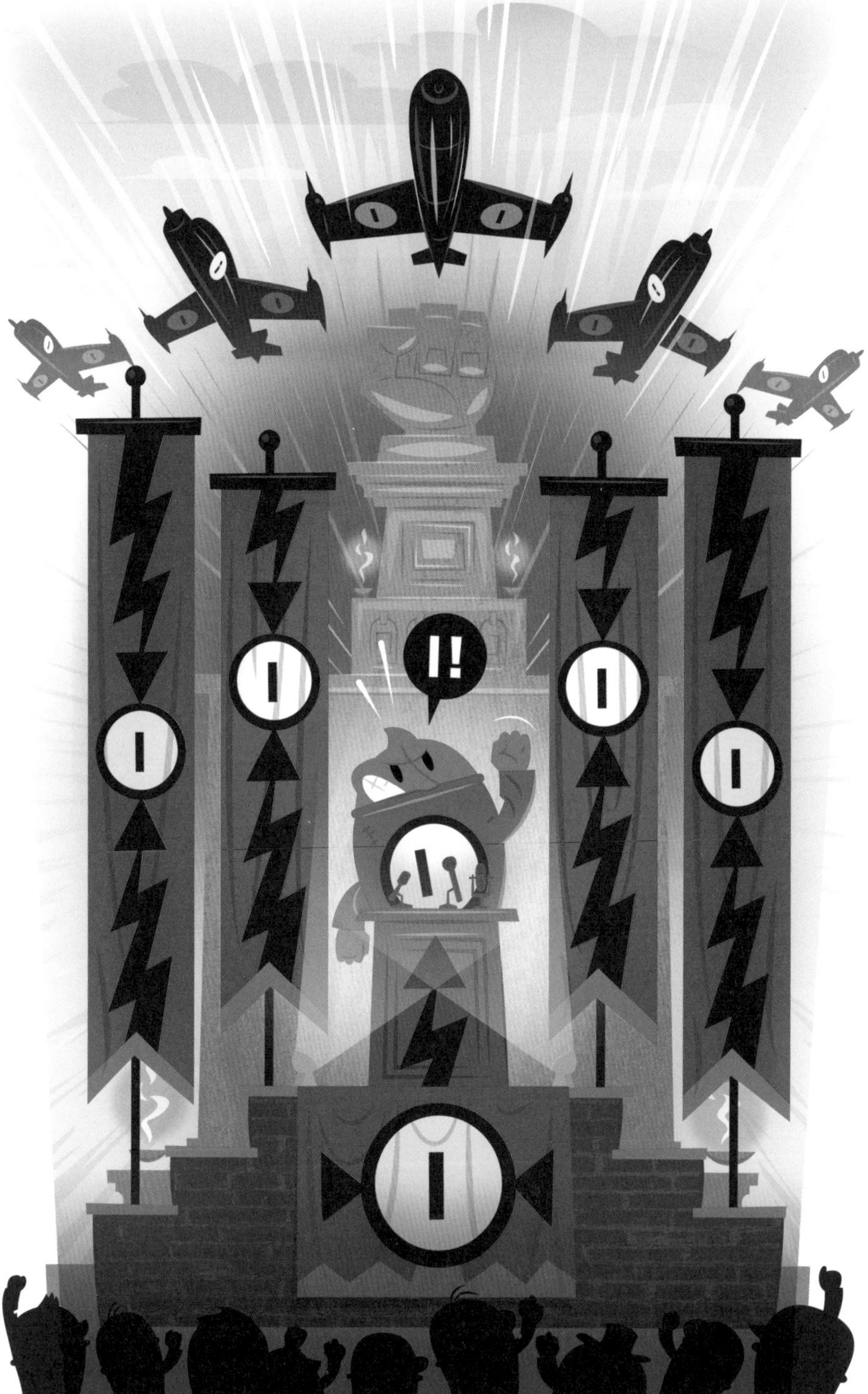
I!

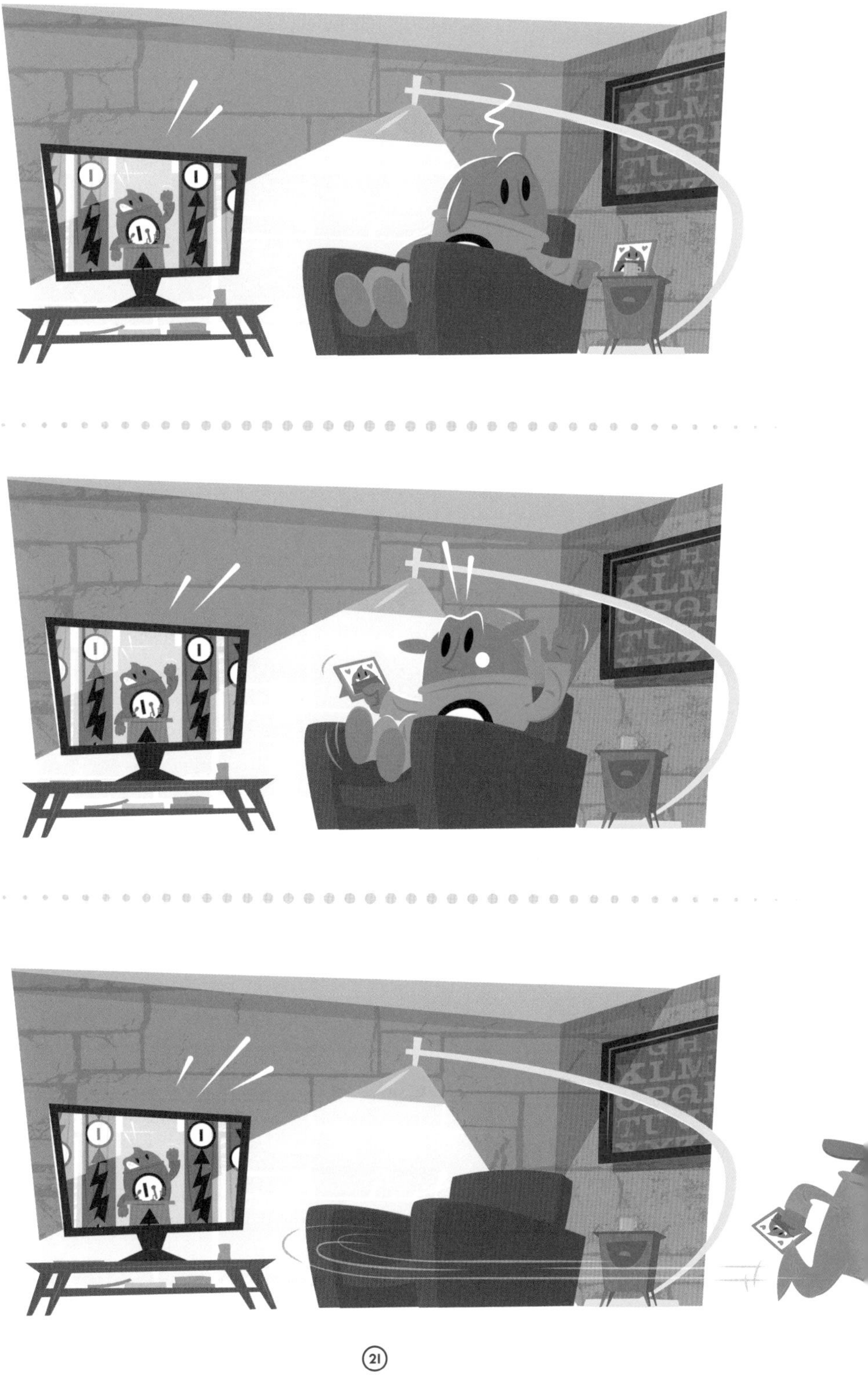

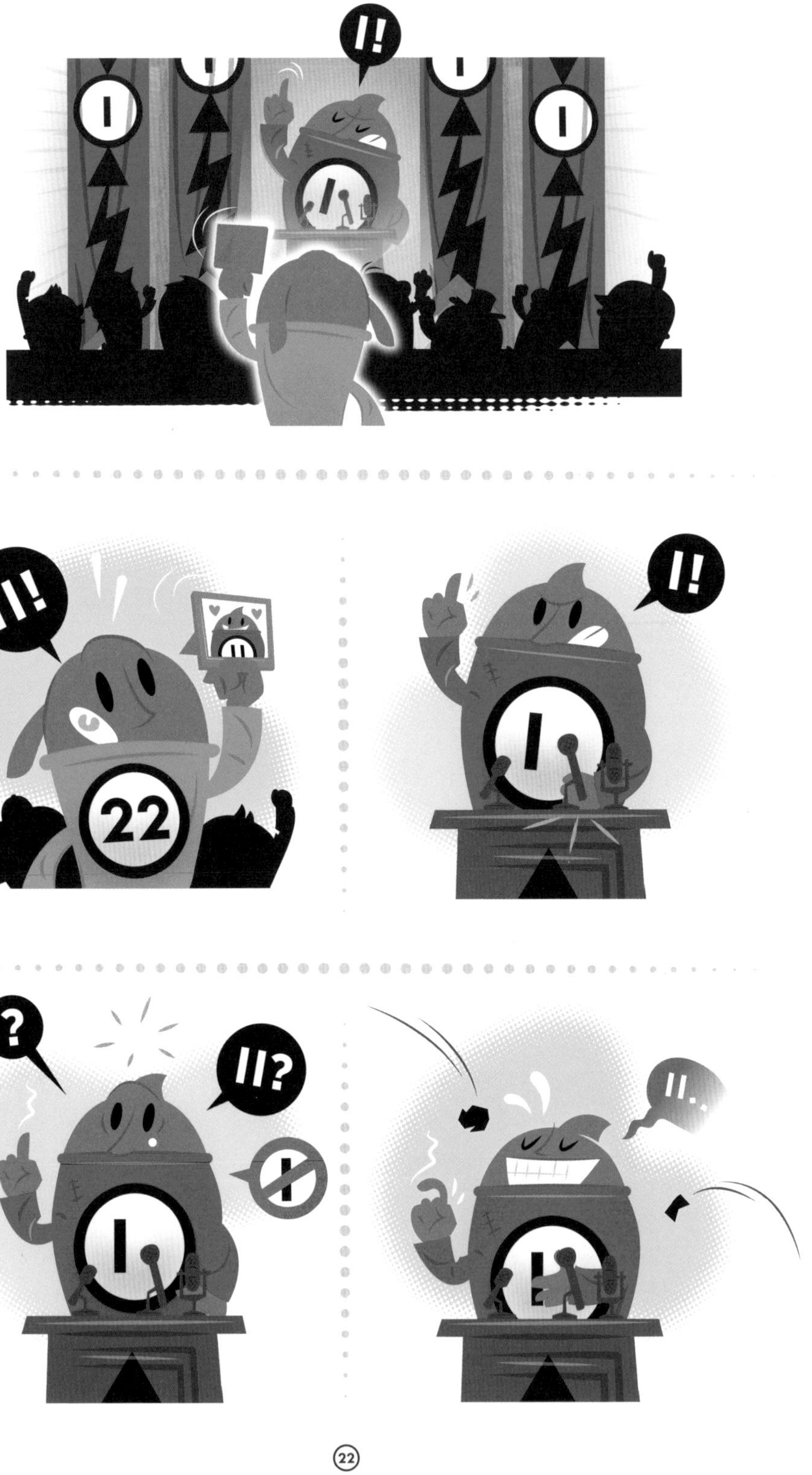
I!
II!
22
I!
?
II?
II..

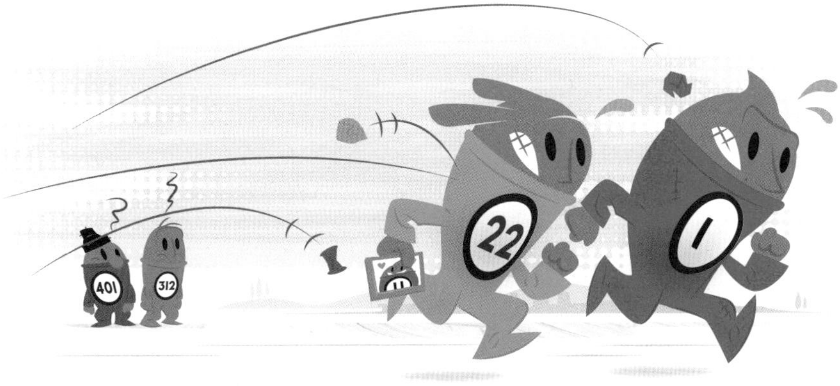
401
312
22
1

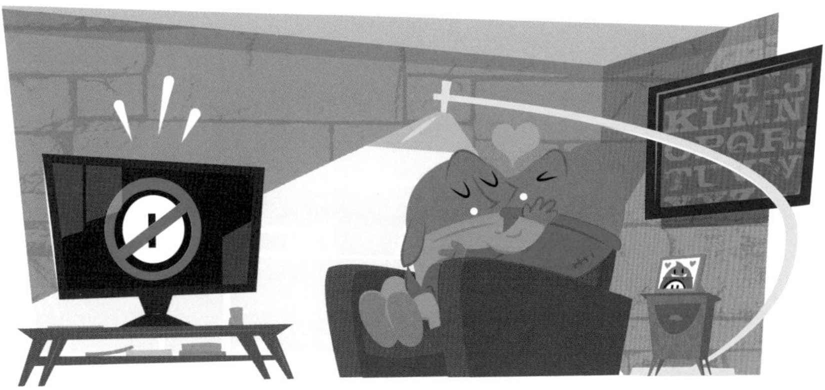

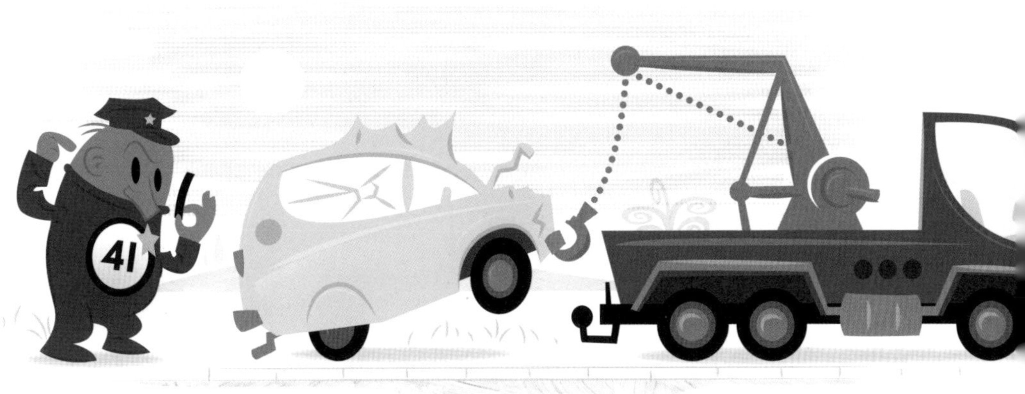
41

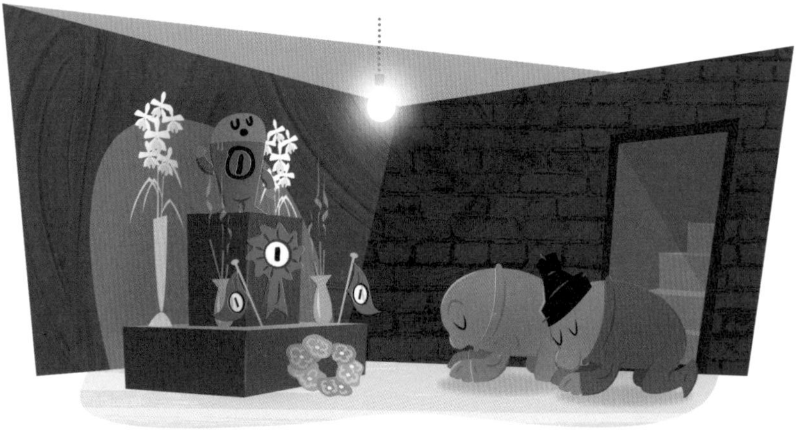

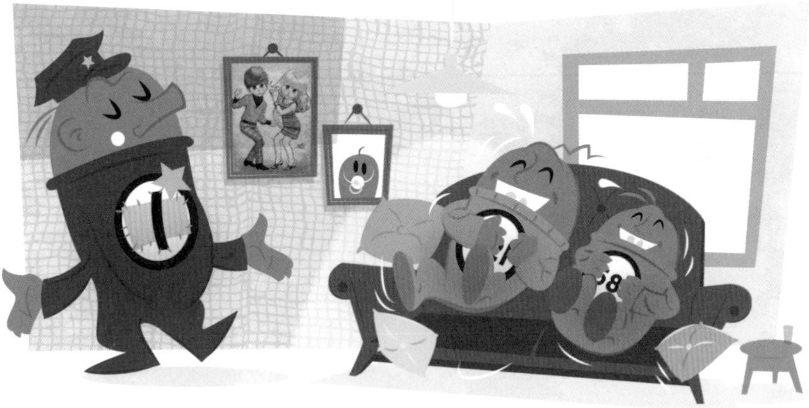

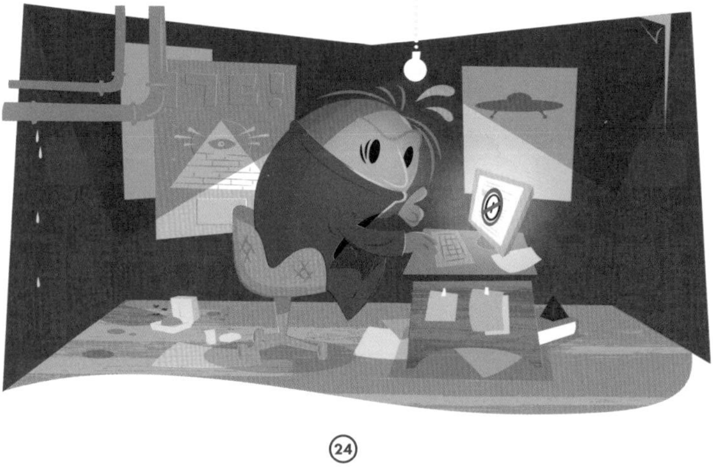

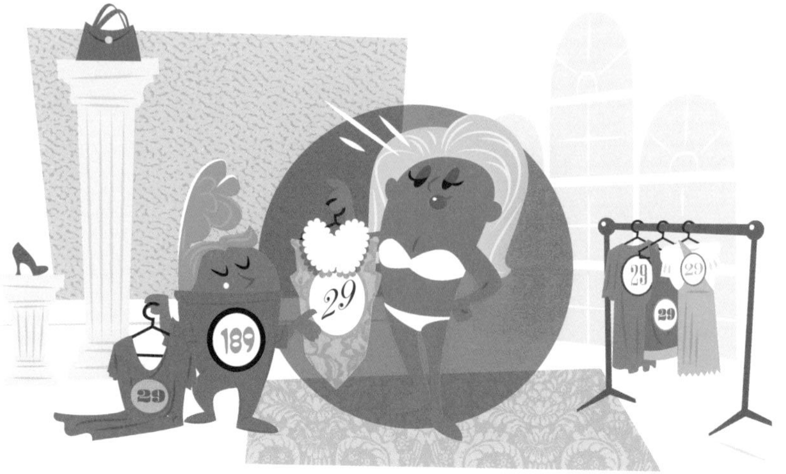
189
29

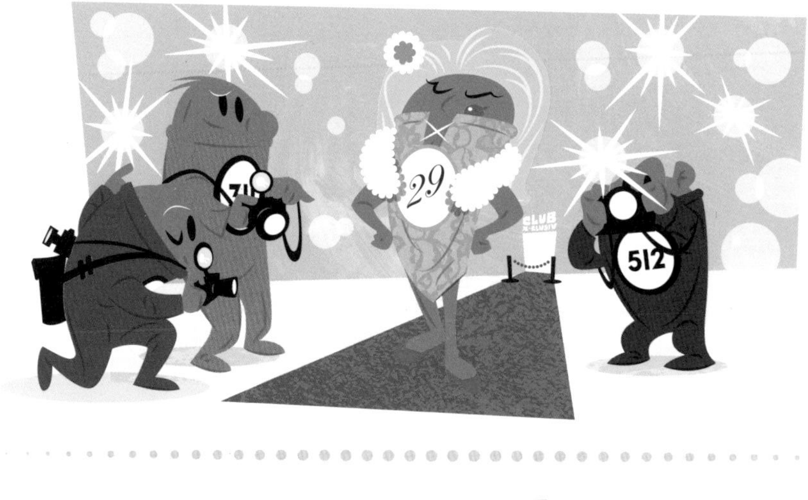
29
512
CLUB

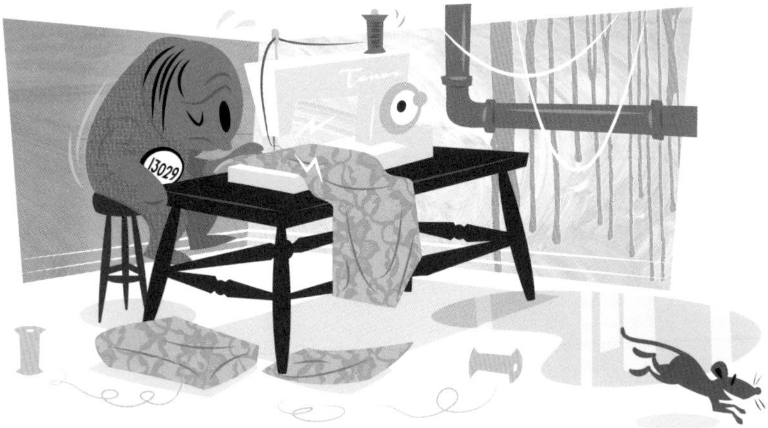
13029

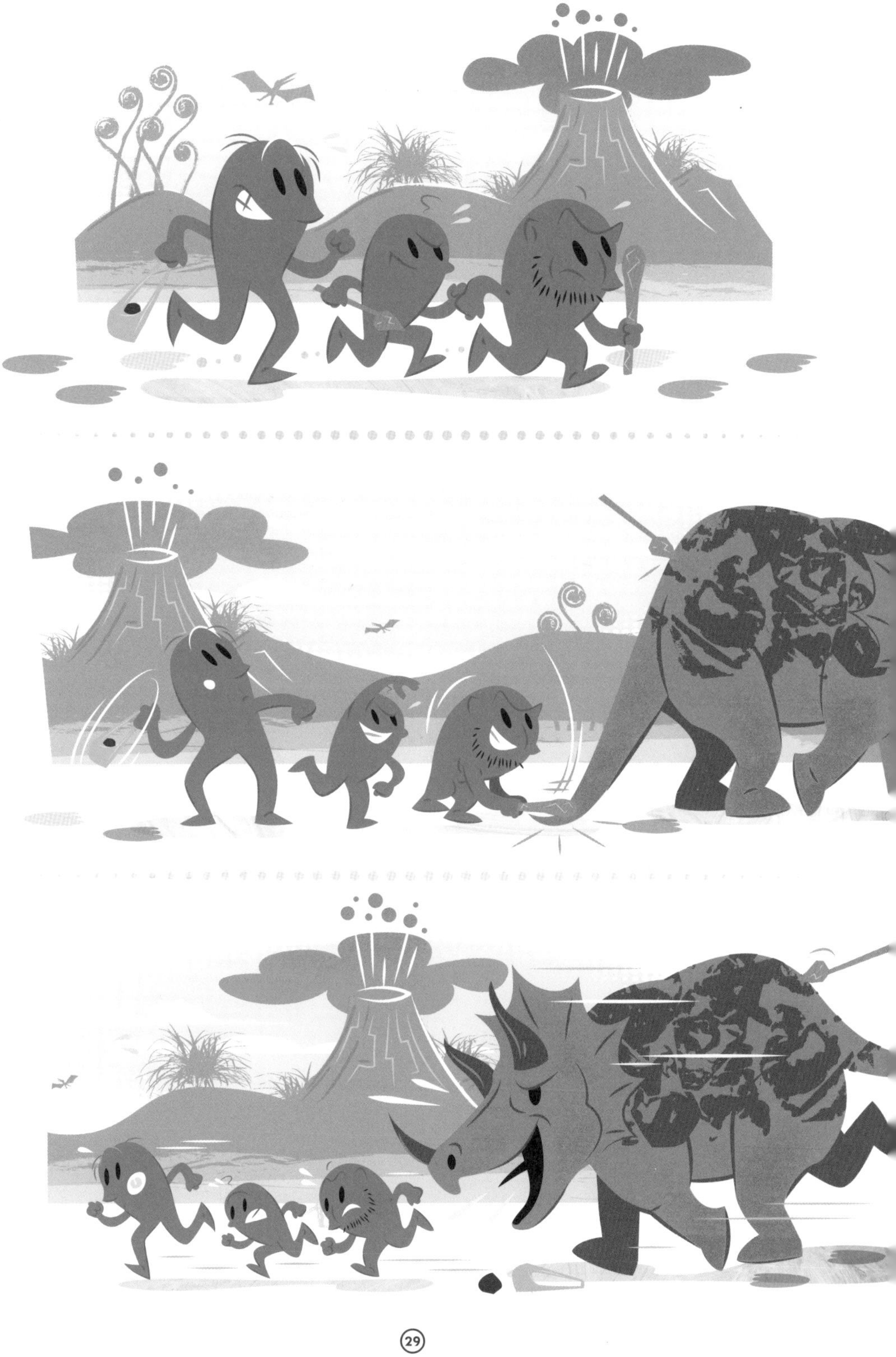

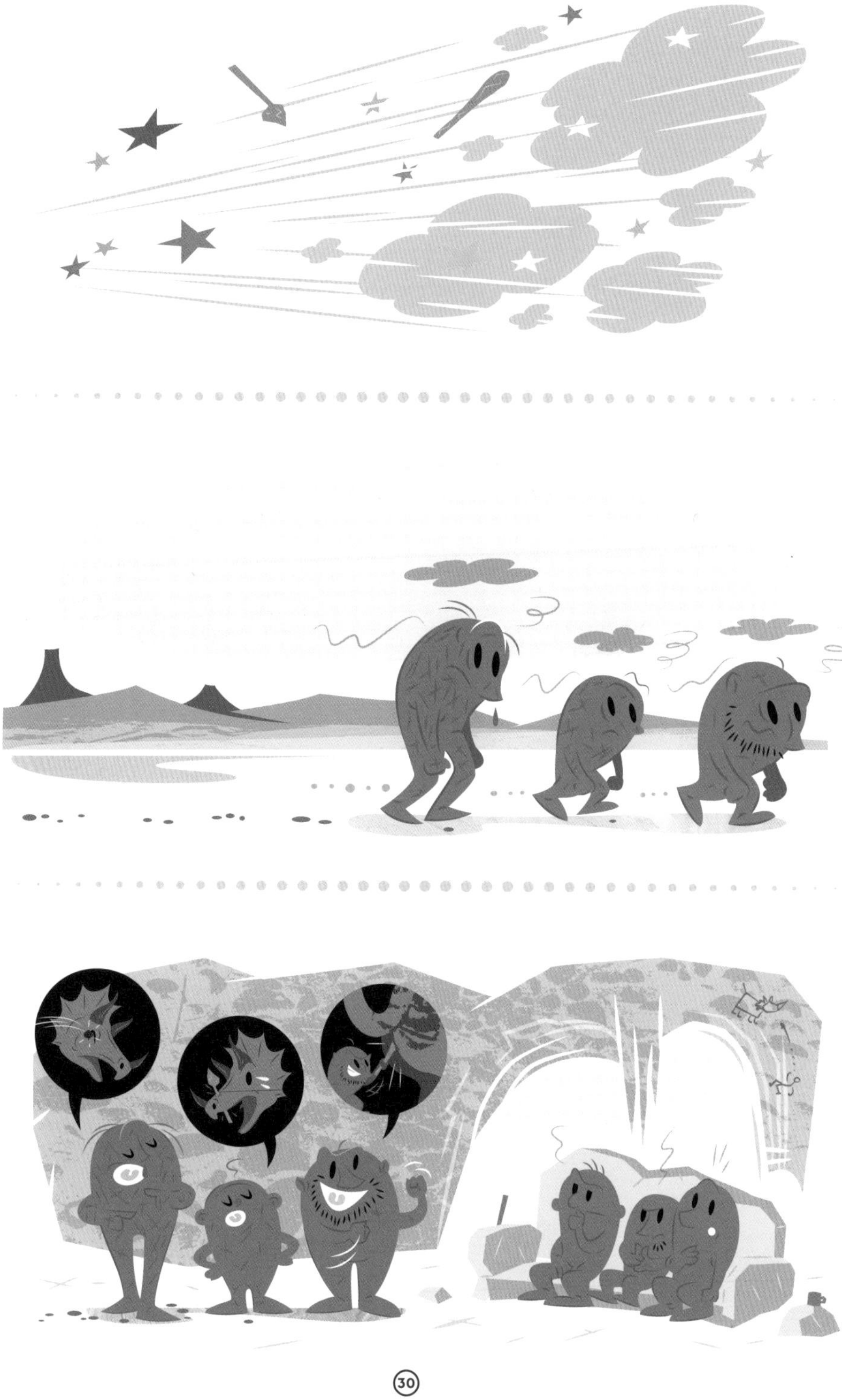

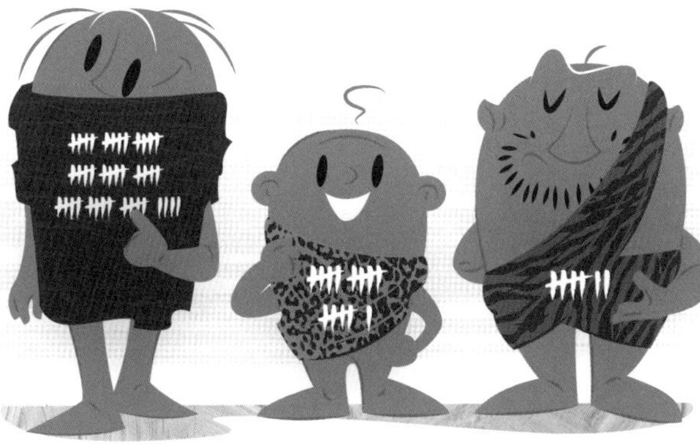

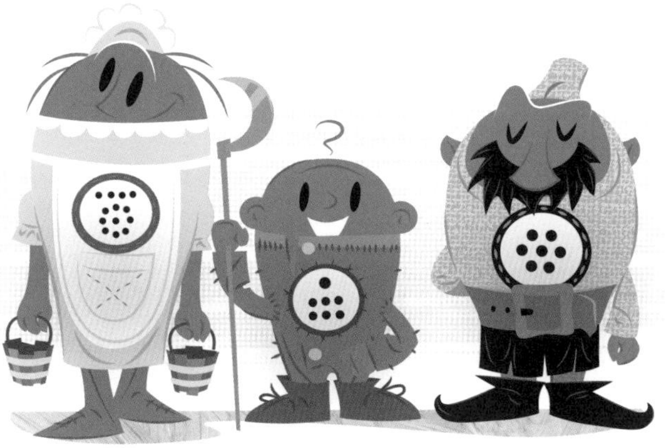

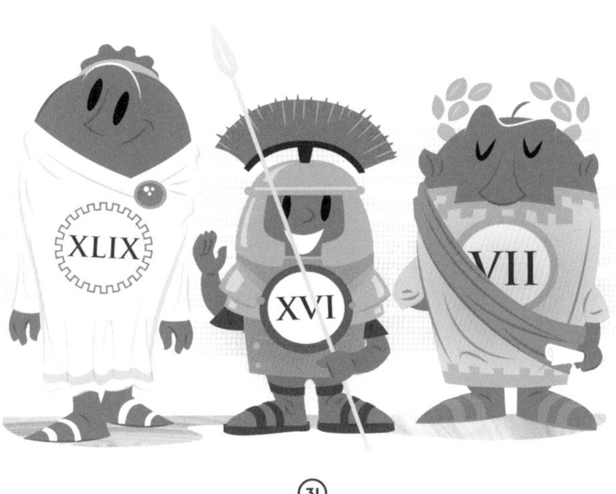
XLIX
XVI
VII

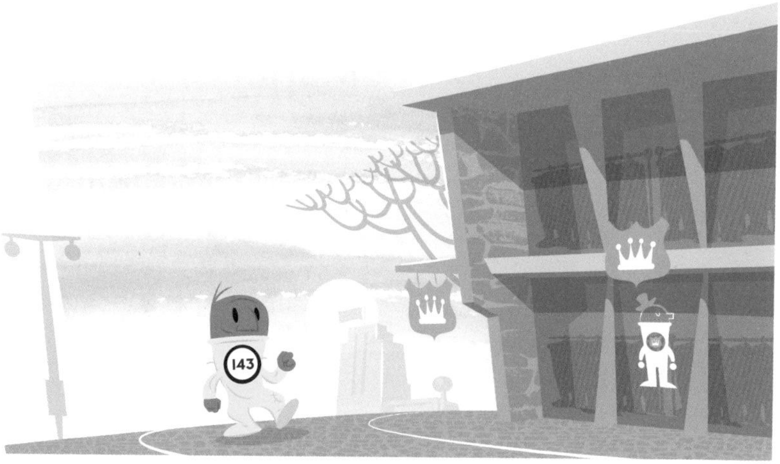
143

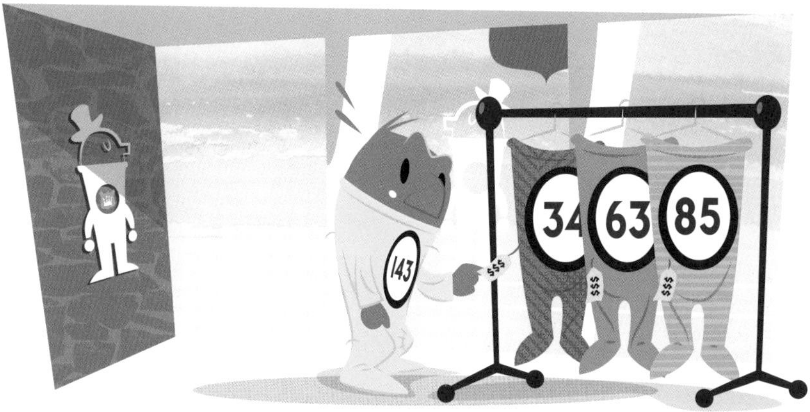
143
$$$
34
63
85
$$$
$$$

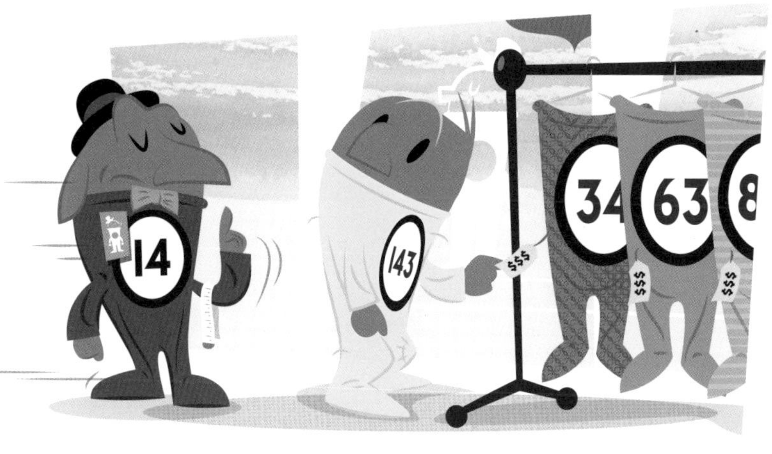
14
143
$$$
34
63
$$$
$$$

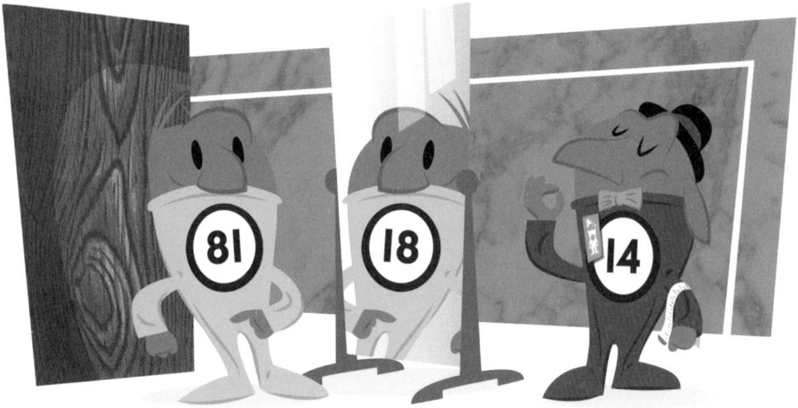

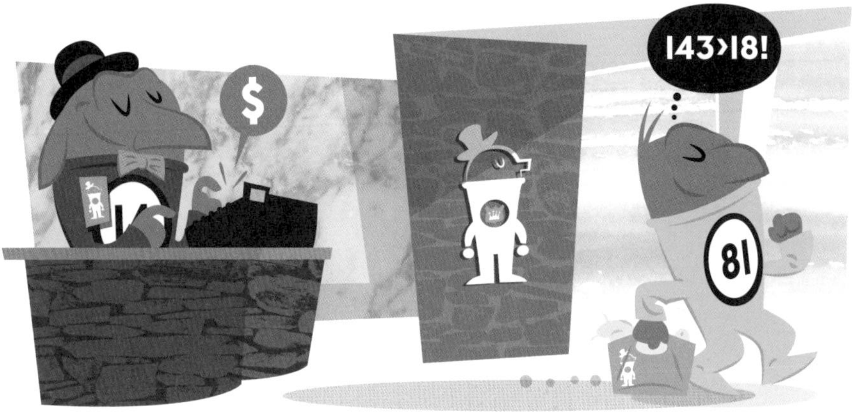
$
143>18!

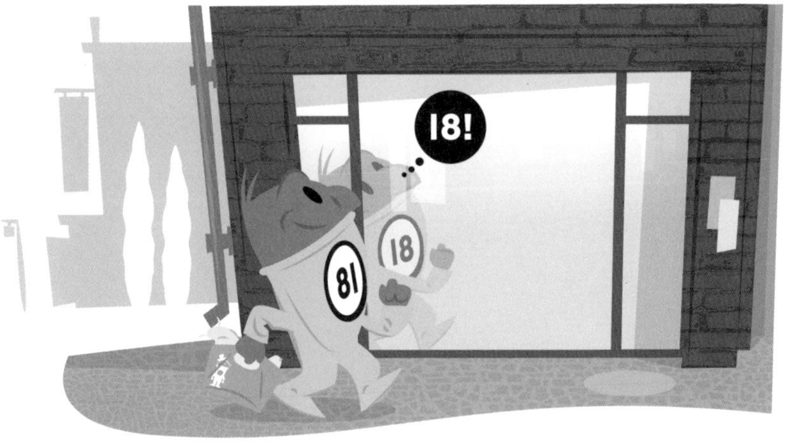
18!

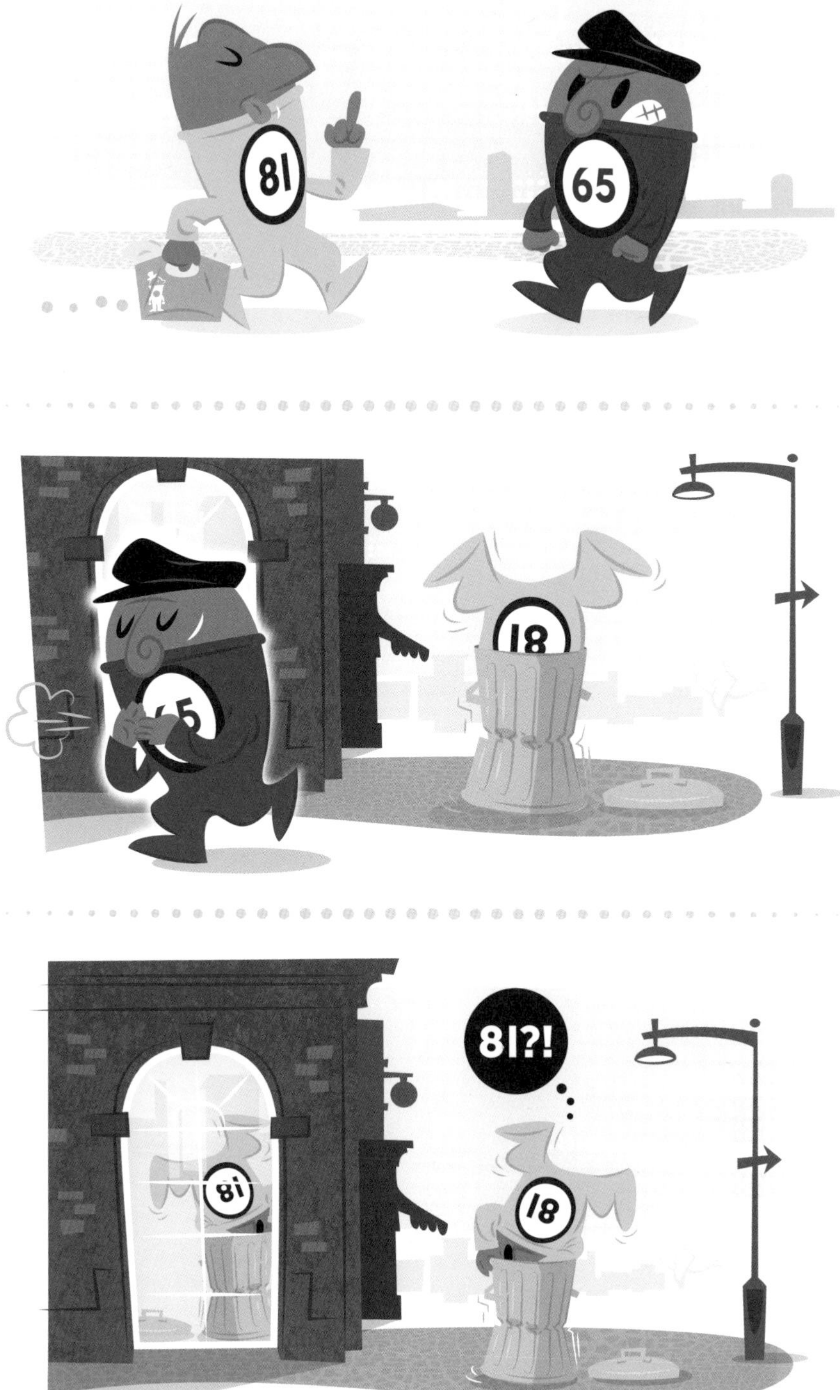
81
65
18
81?!
18

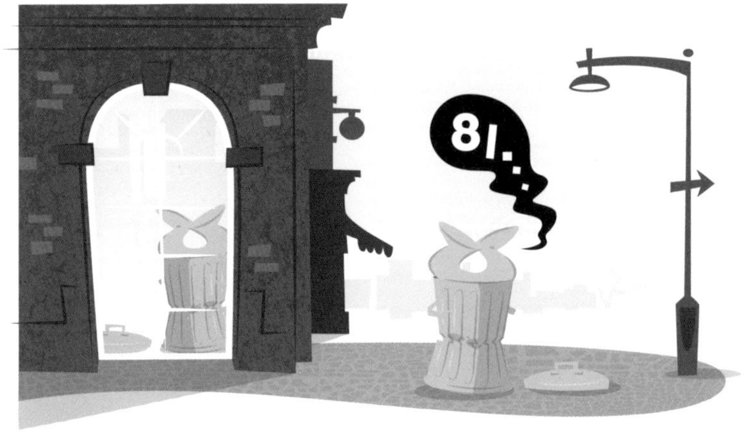
81...

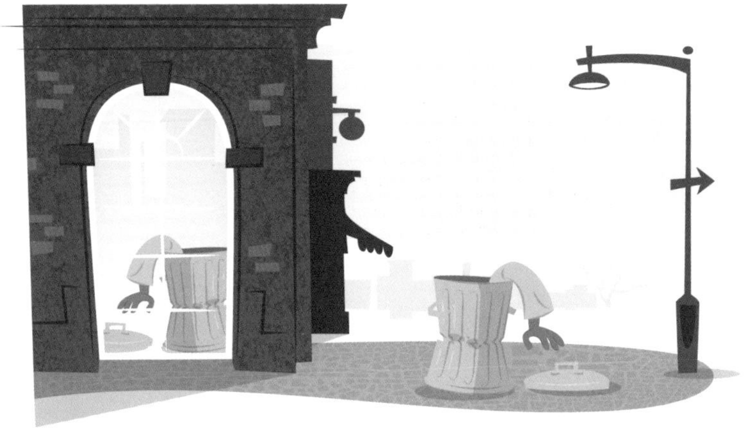

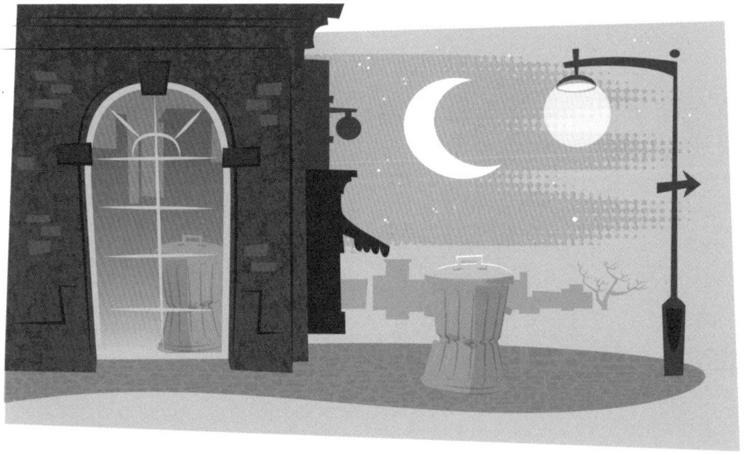

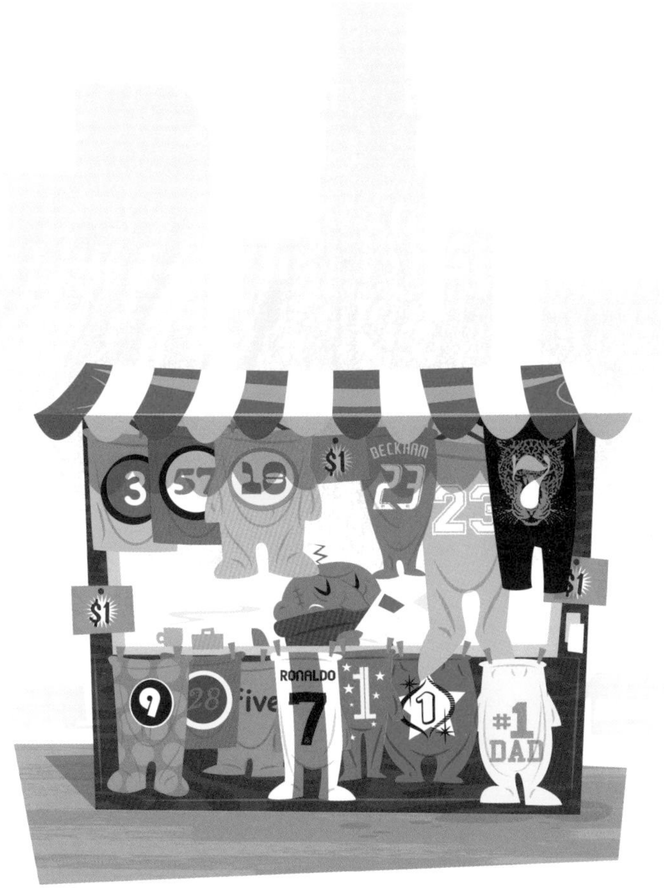
3
57
$1
BECKHAM
23
23
$1
$1
9
28
five
RONALDO
7
1
#1
DAD

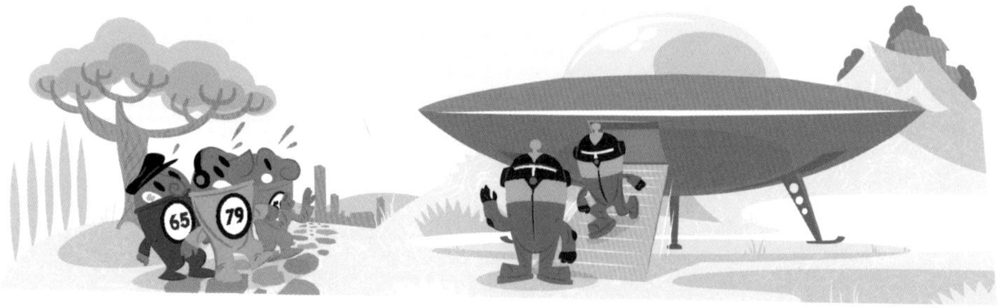
65
79

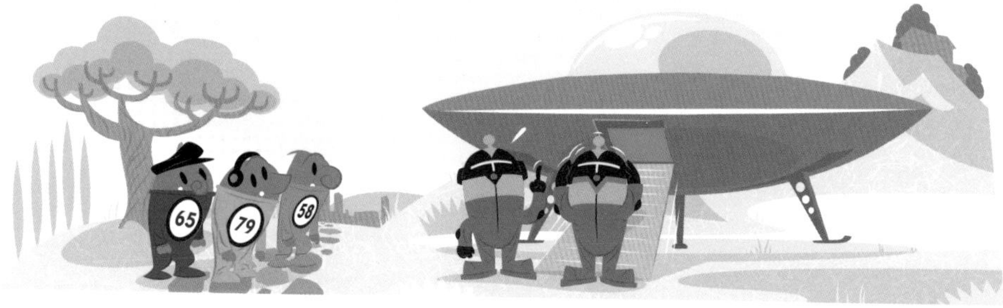
65
79
58

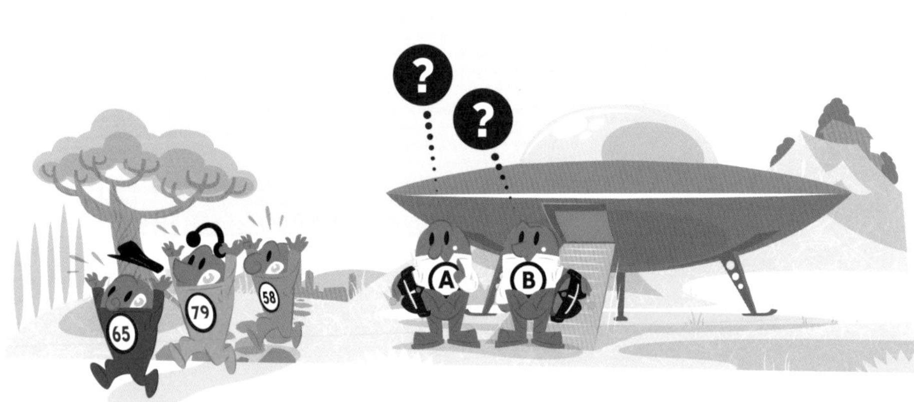
?
?
A
B
65
79
58

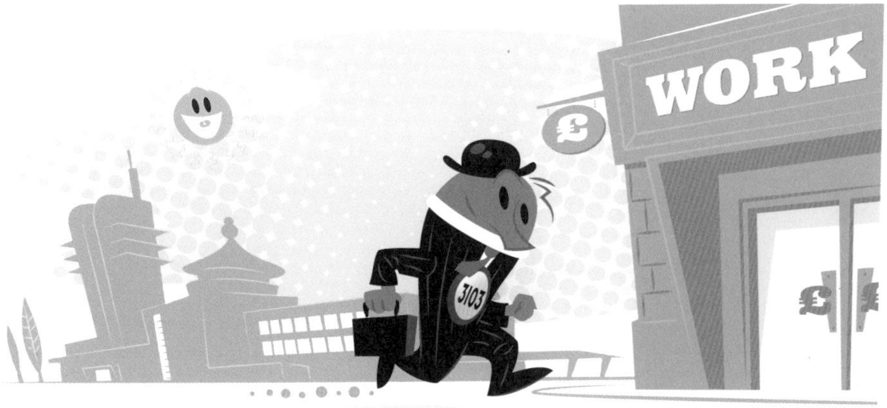
WORK
£
3103

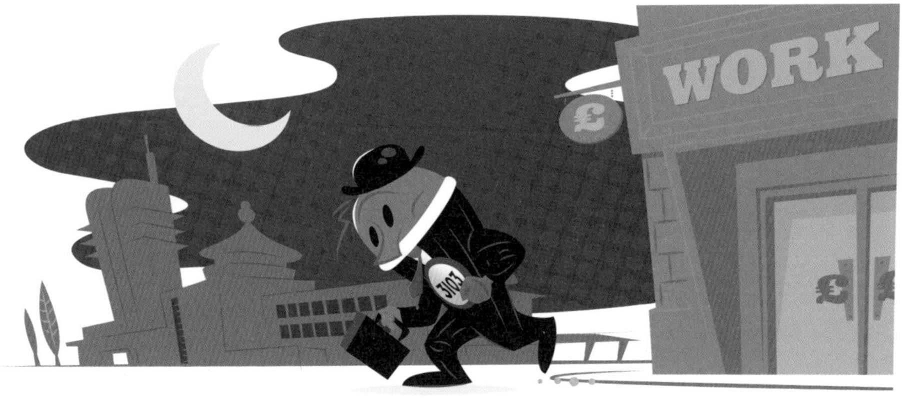
WORK
£
3103

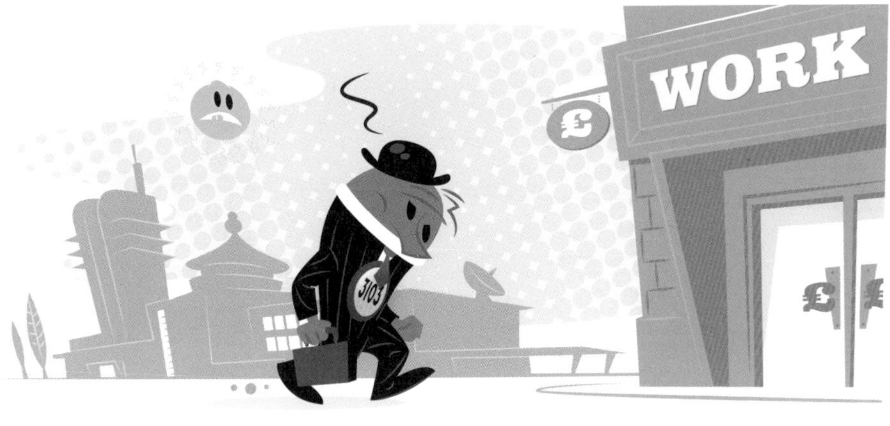
WORK
£
3103

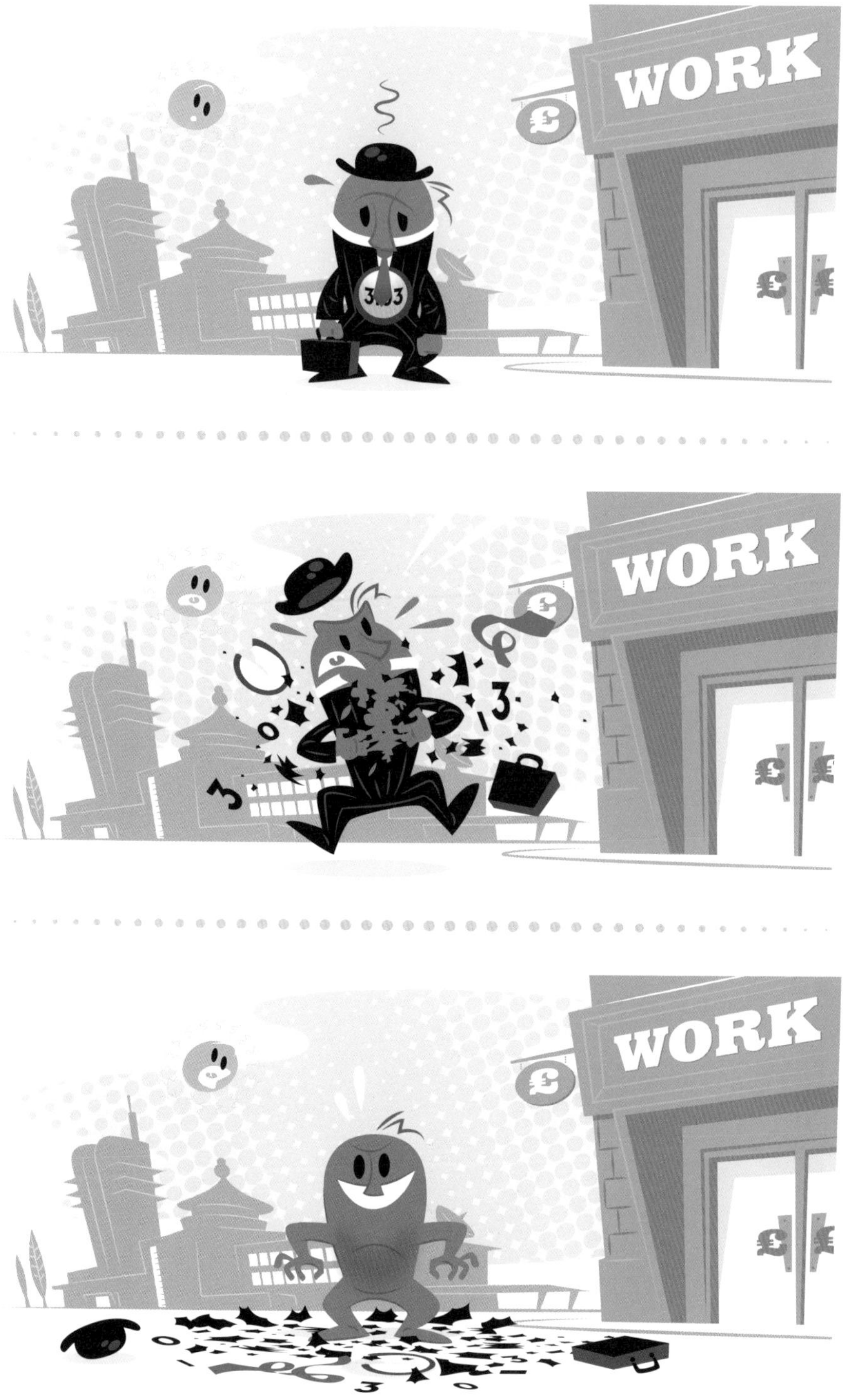
WORK
WORK
WORK

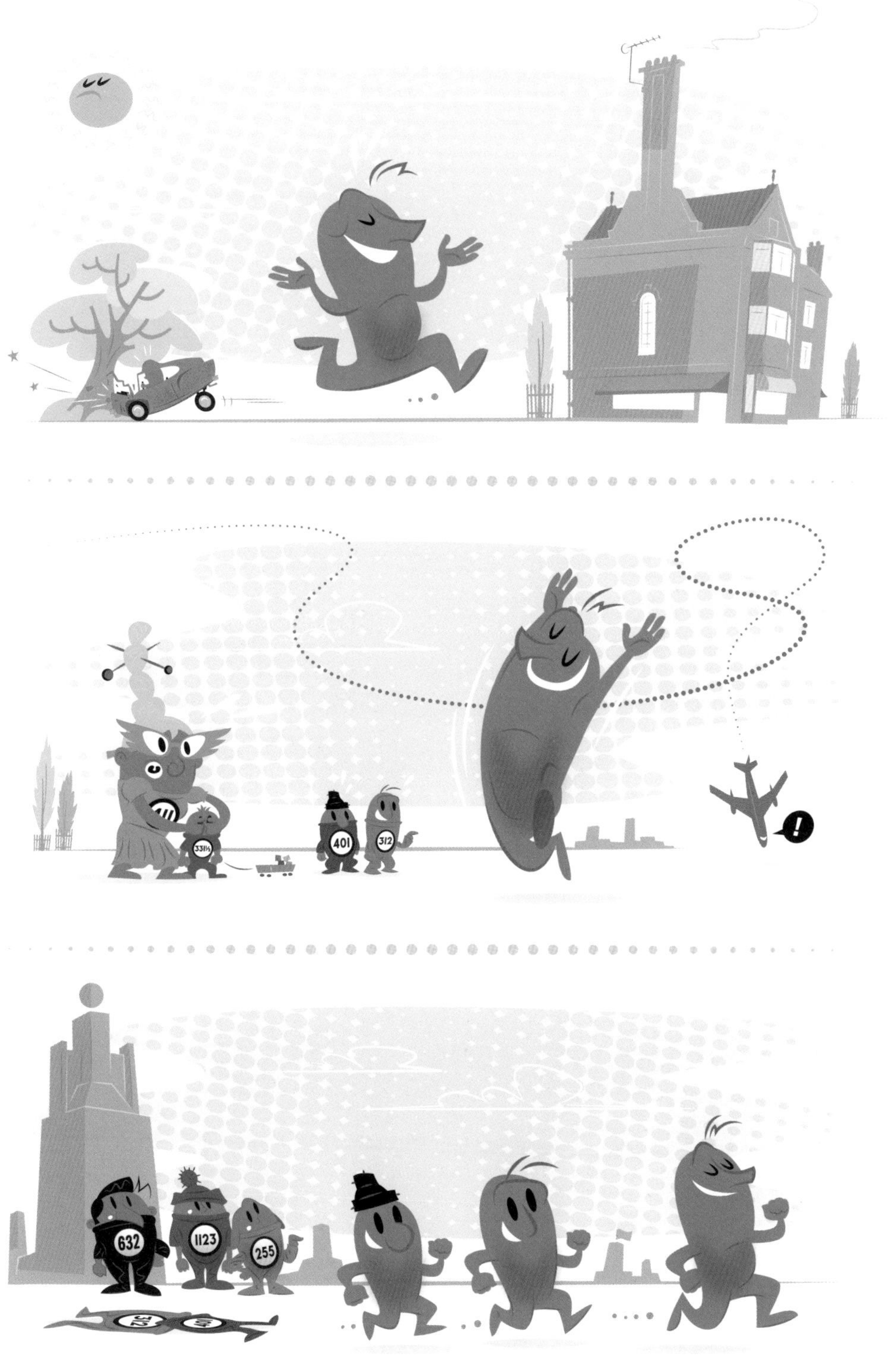
401
312
!
632
1123
255

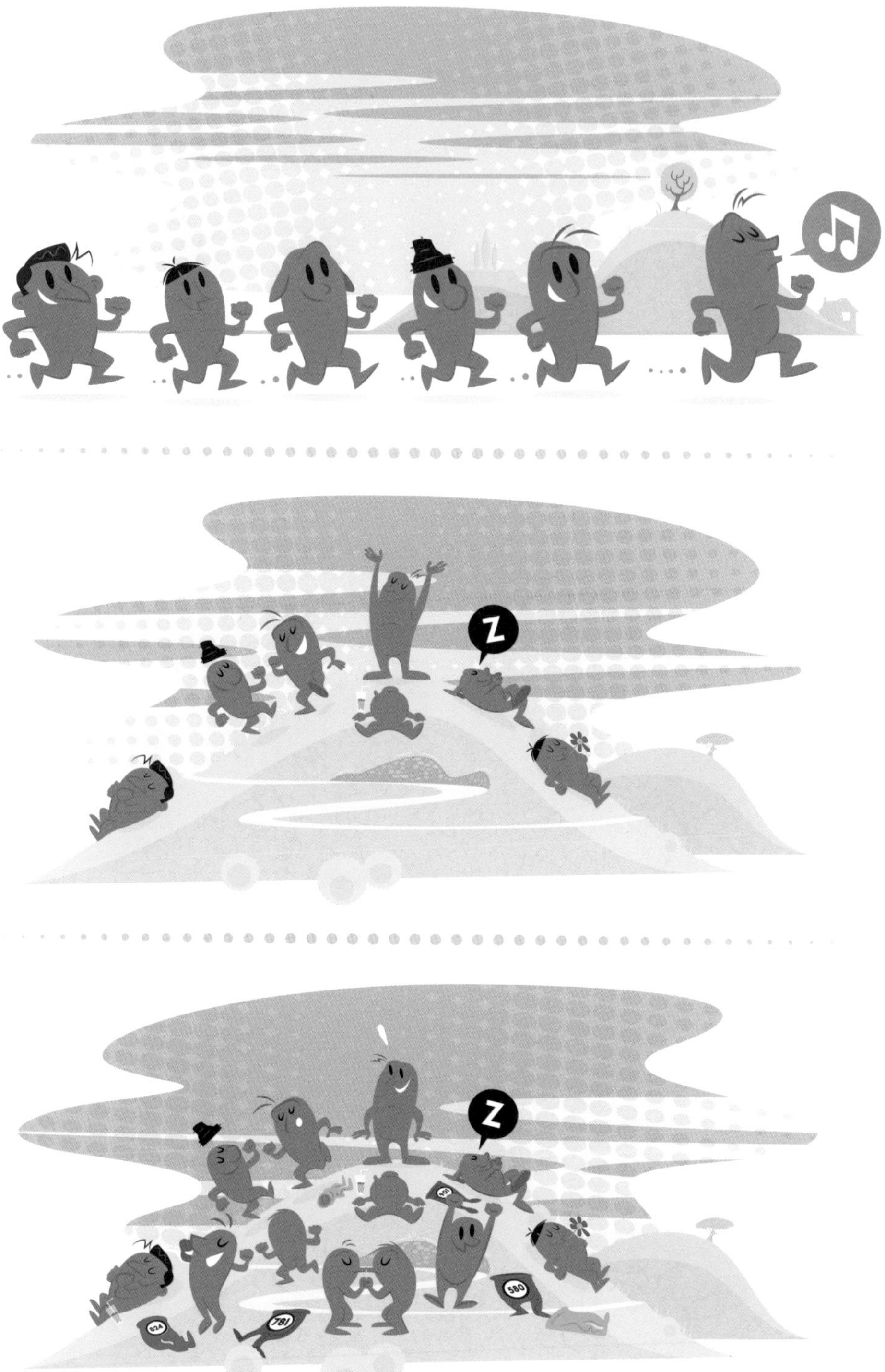
Z
Z

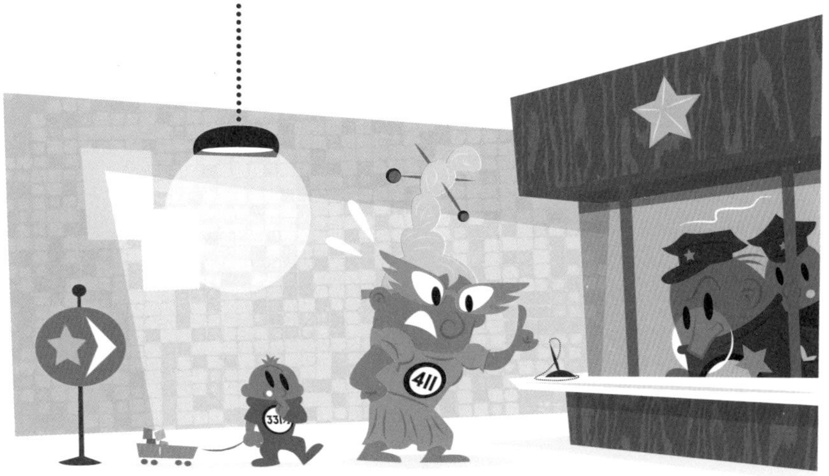
3319
411

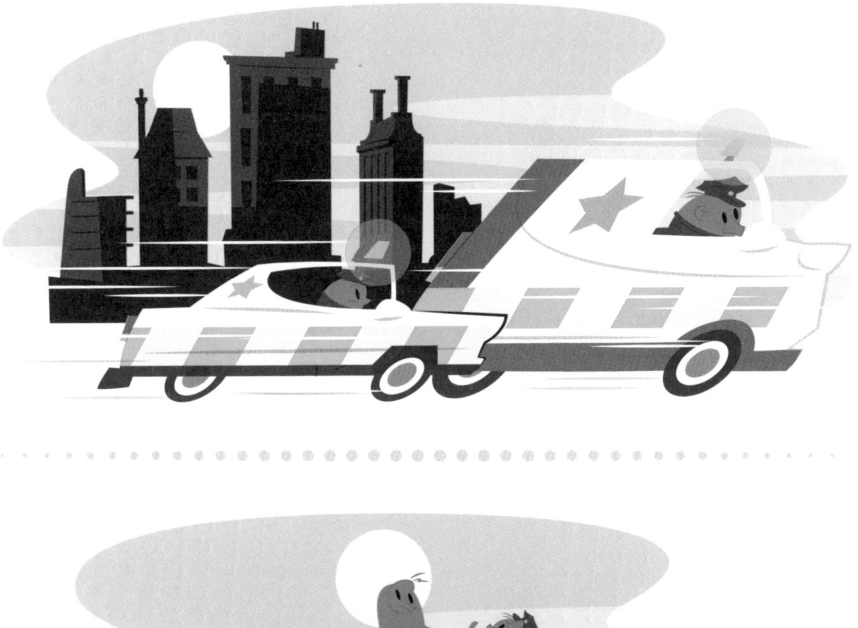

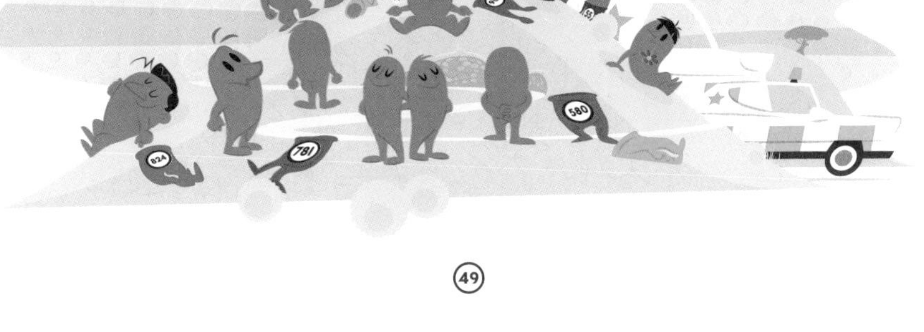
41
824
781
580

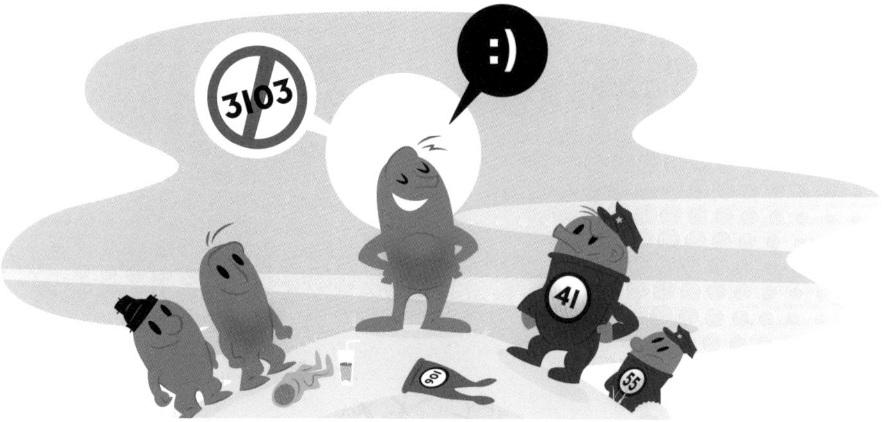
3103
:)
41
55

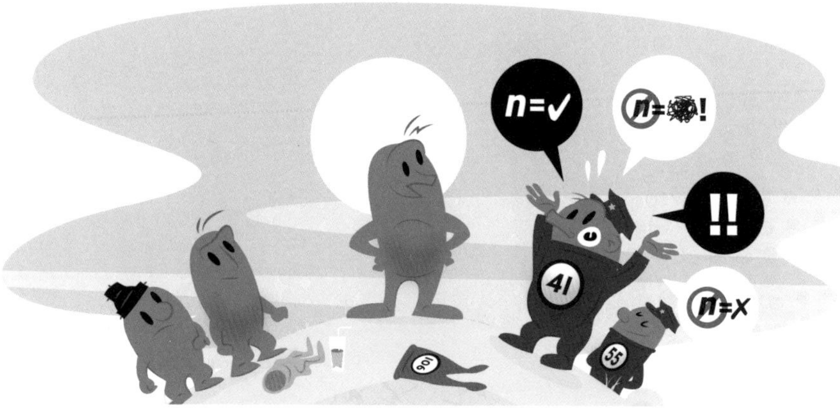
n=✓
!
!!
n=✗
41
55

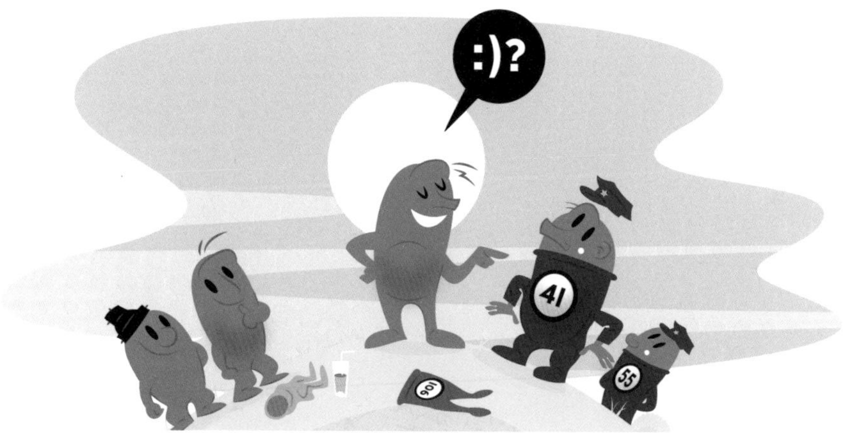
:)?
41
55

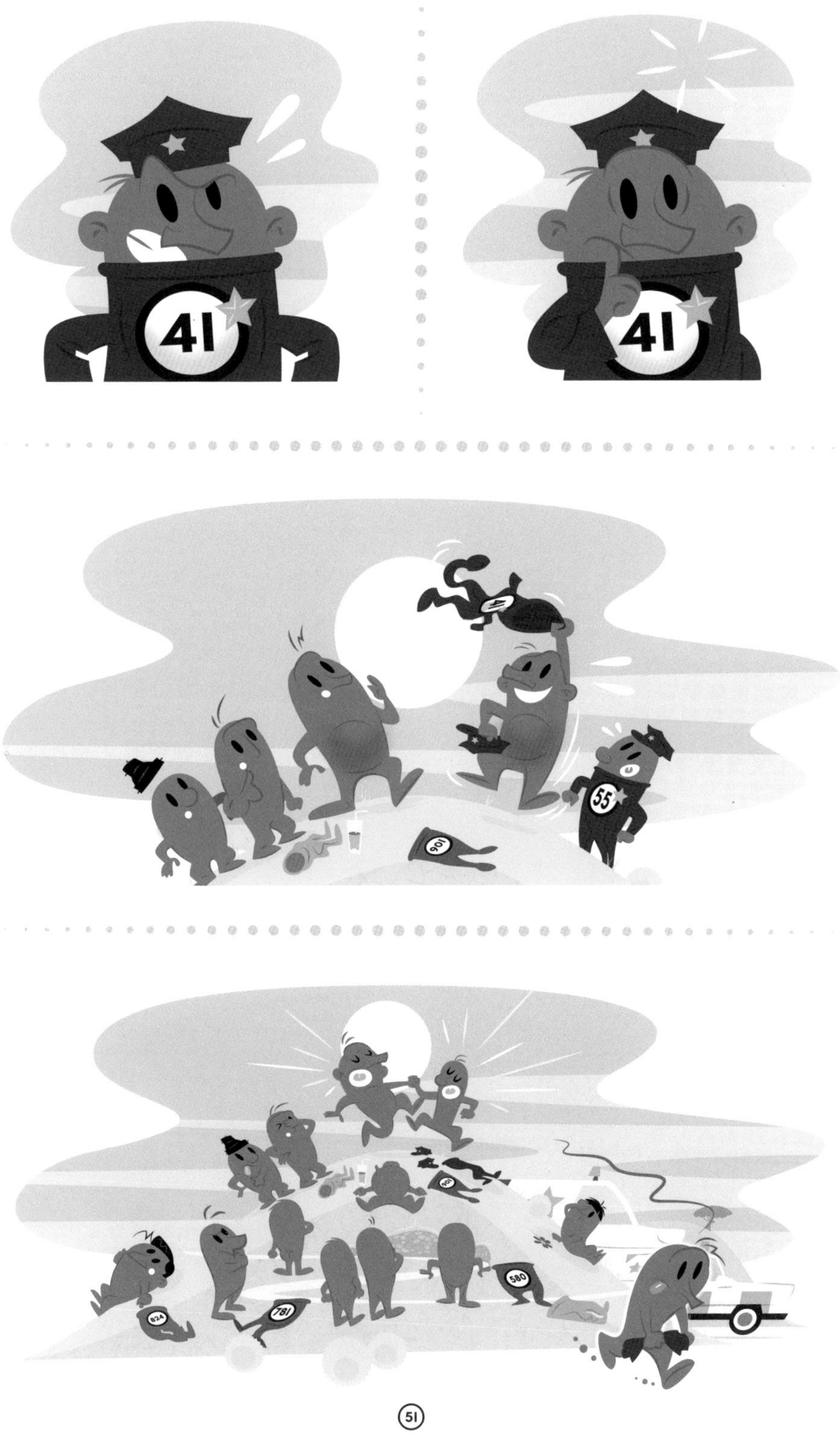
41
41
55
106
580
781
824

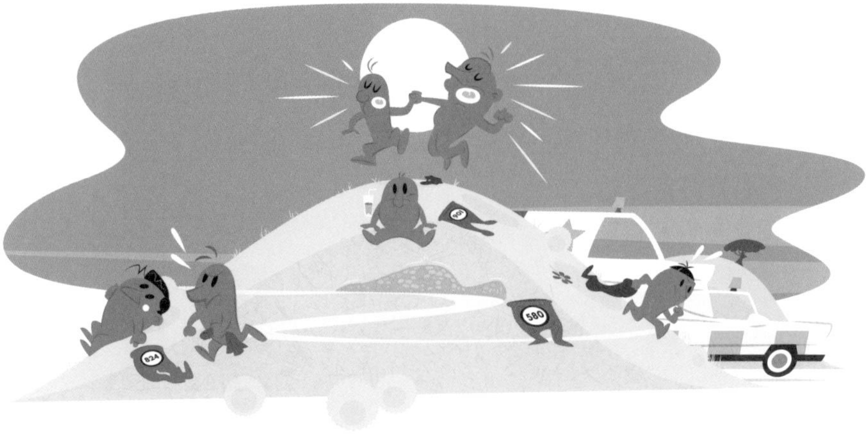
824
580

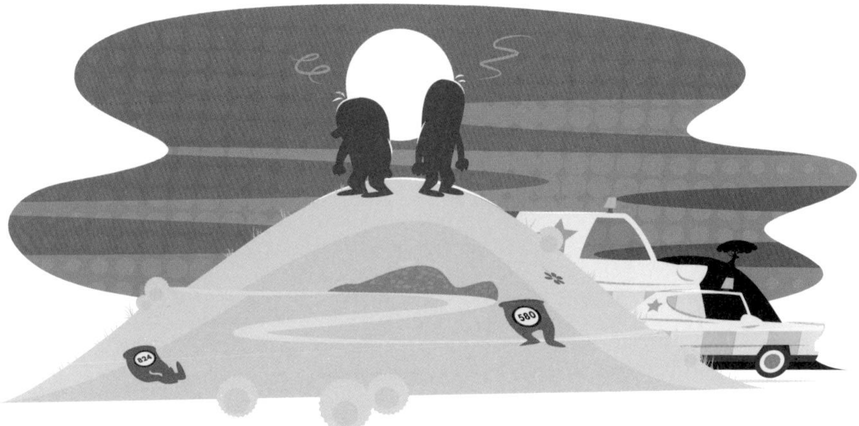
824
580

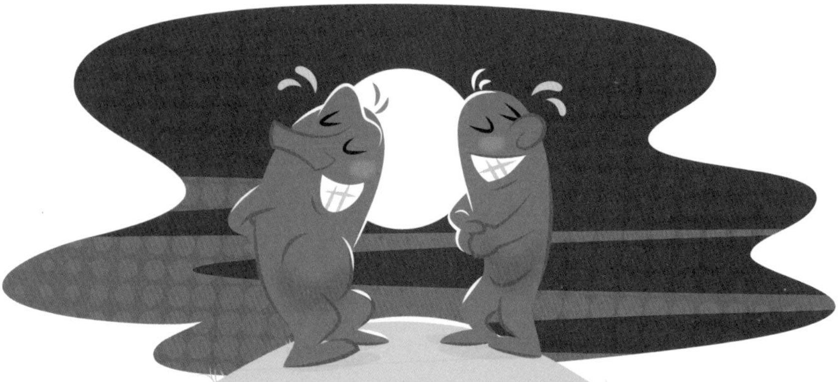

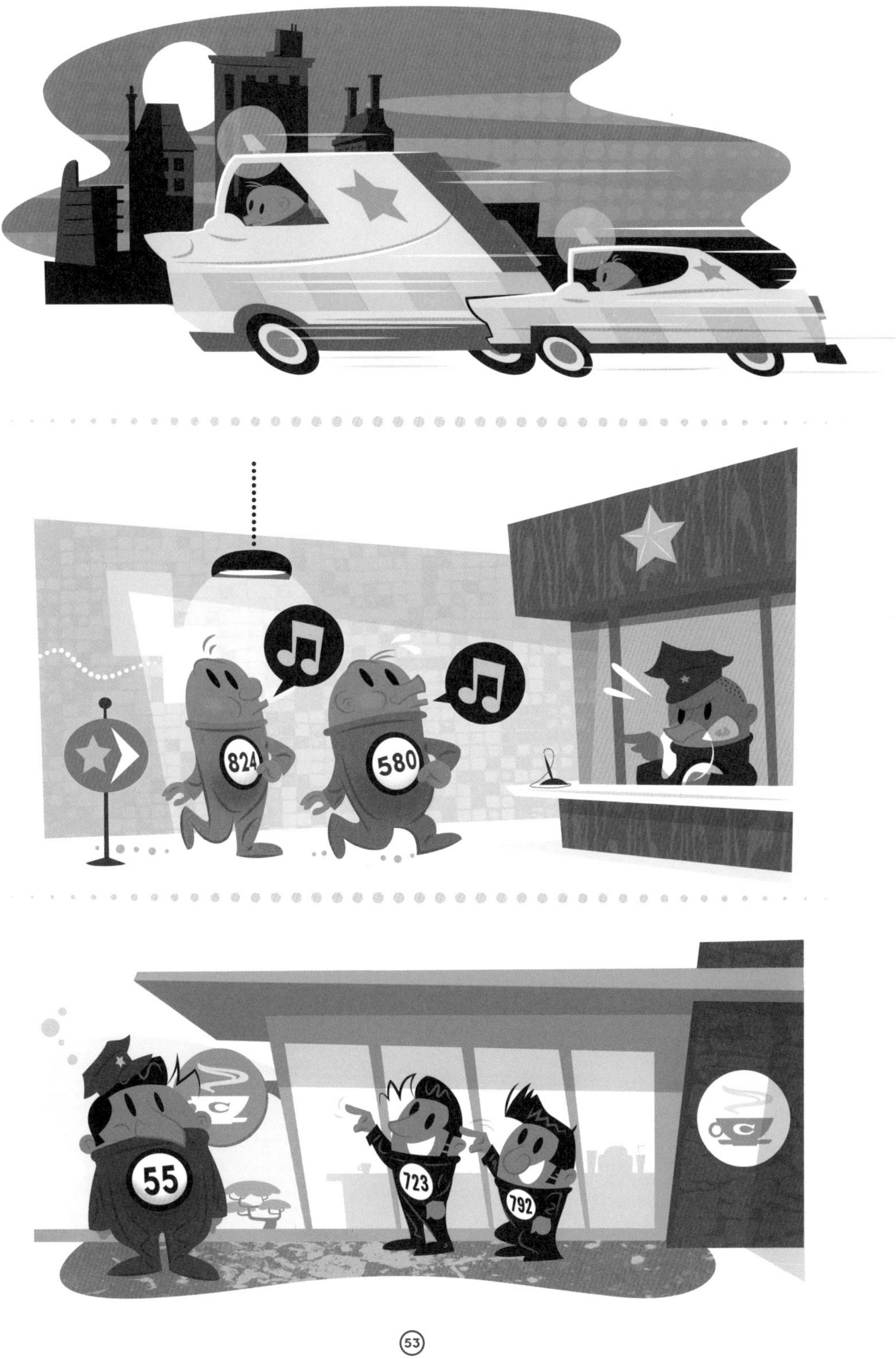
824
580
55
723
792

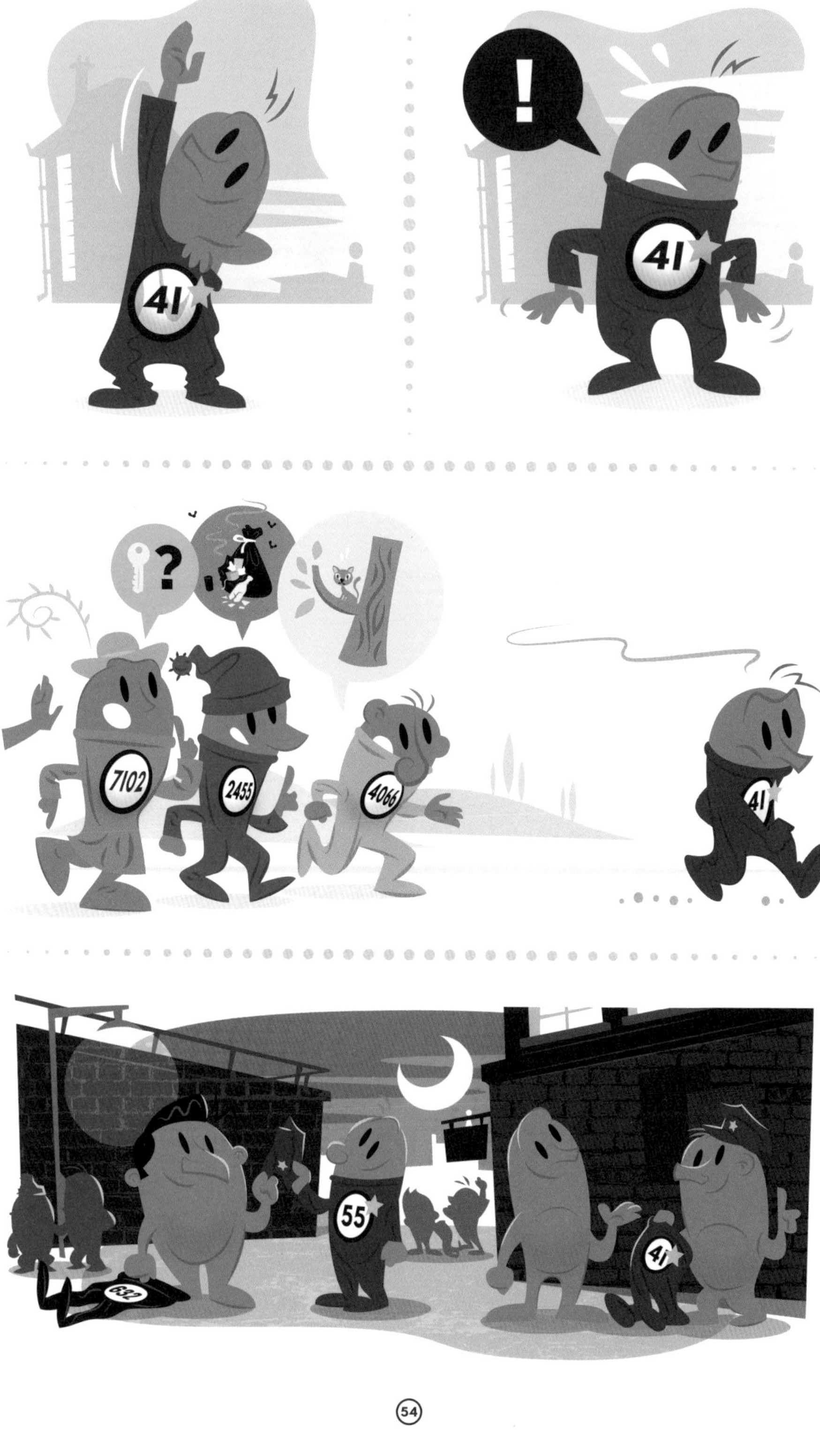
41
!
41
?
7102
2455
4066
41
632
55
41

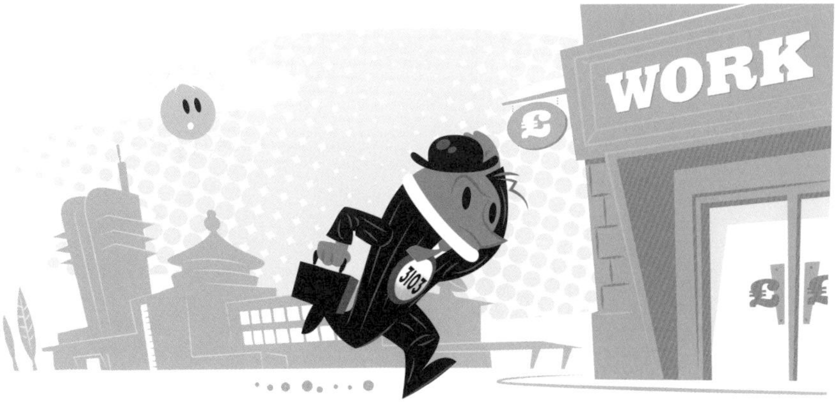
WORK
£
3103

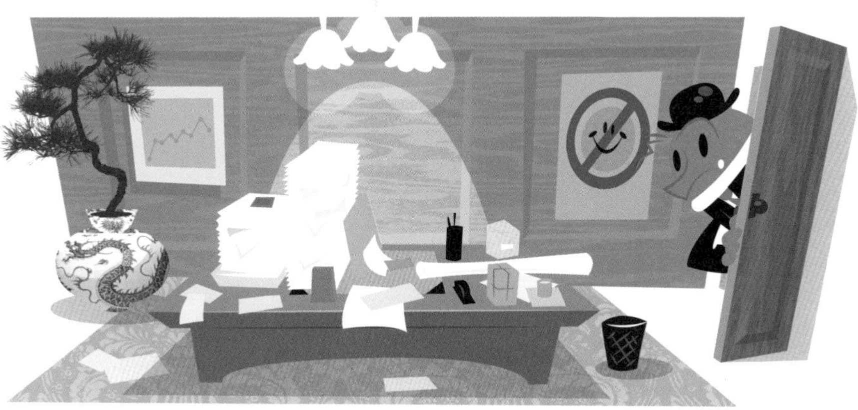

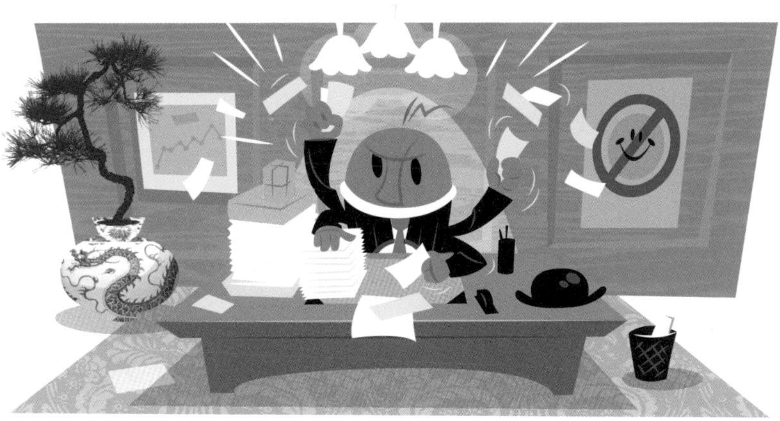

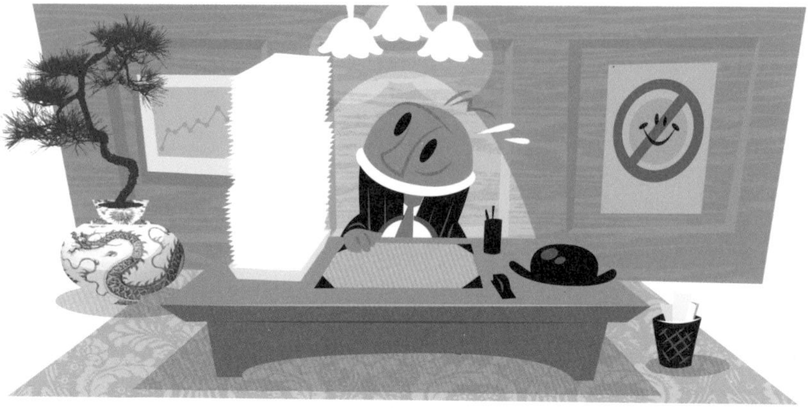

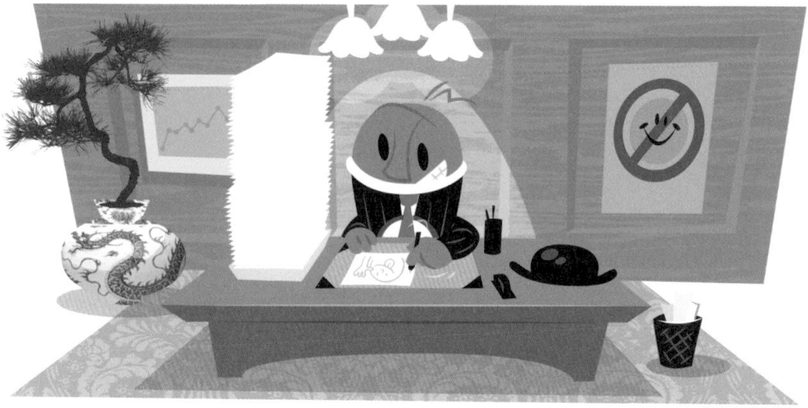

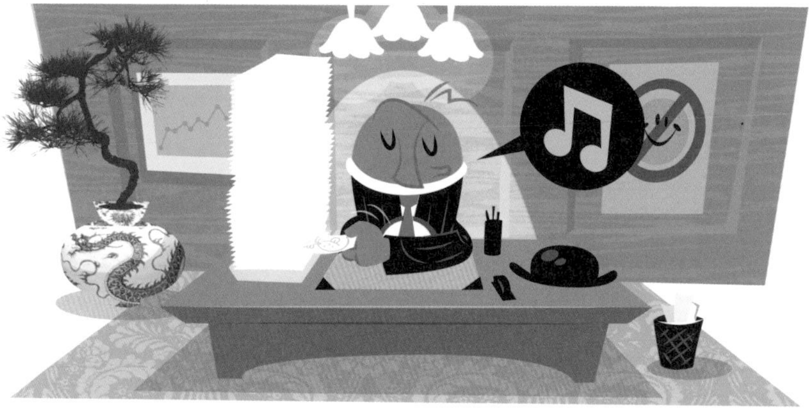

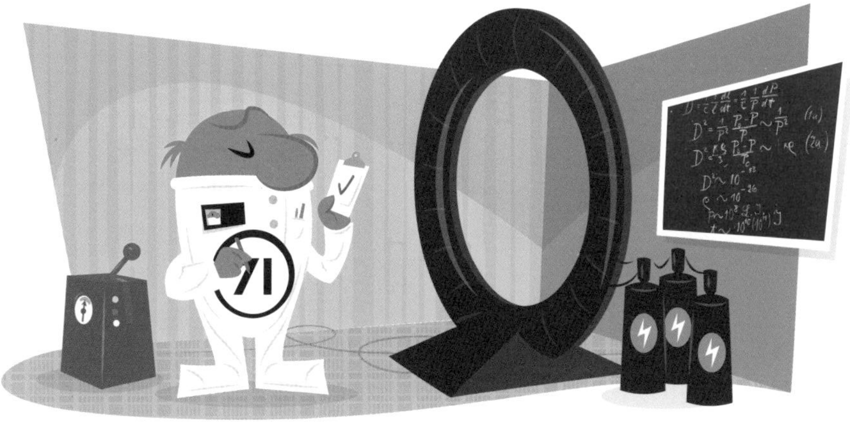

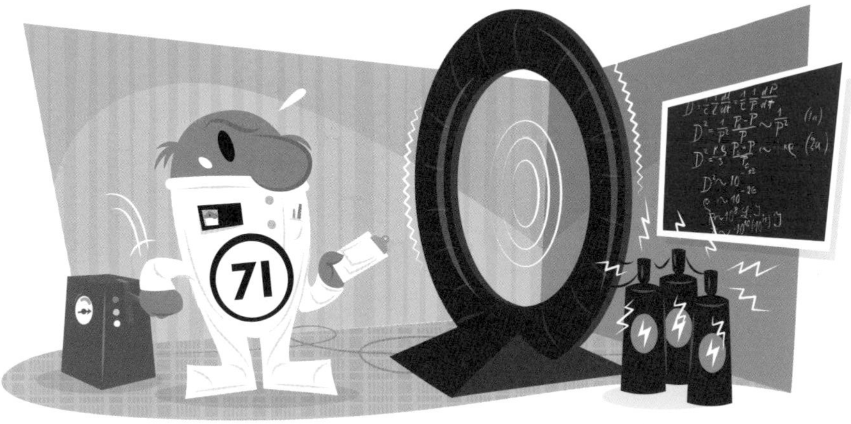

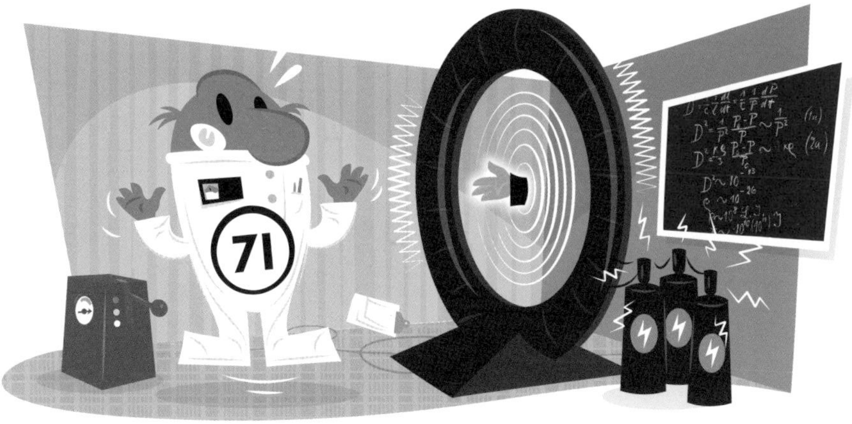

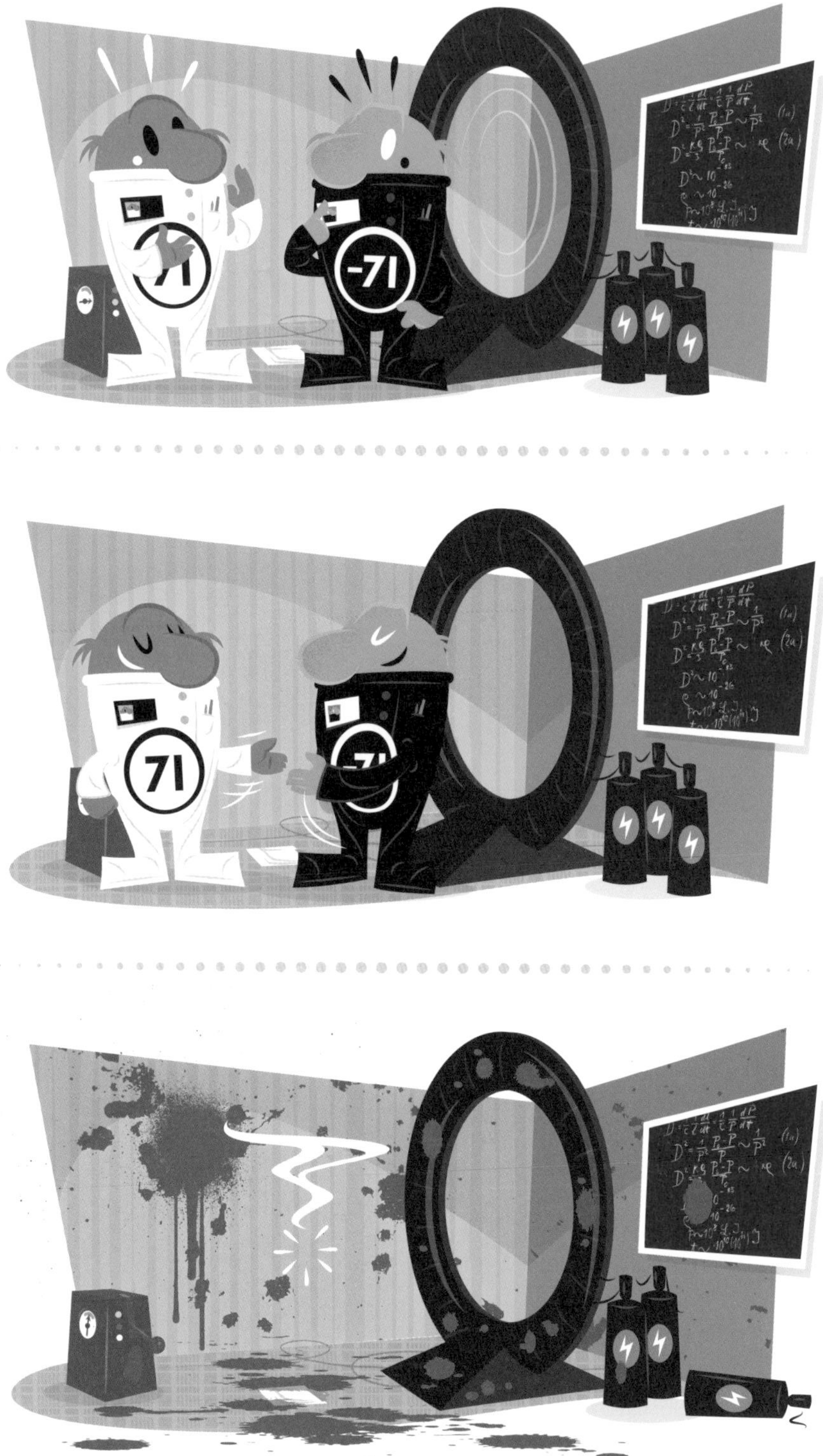
71
-71
71
-71

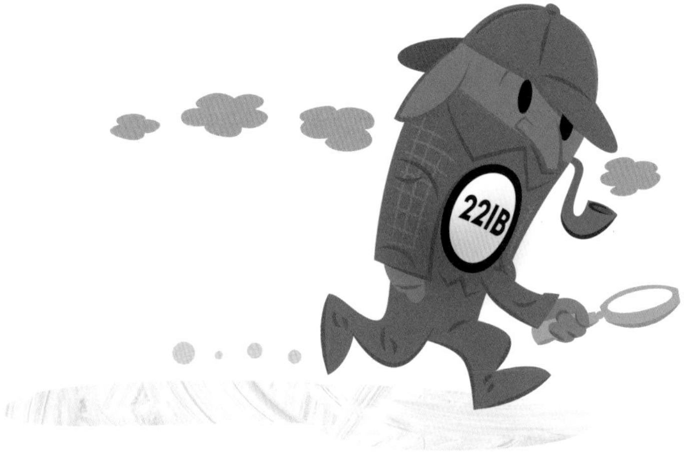
221B

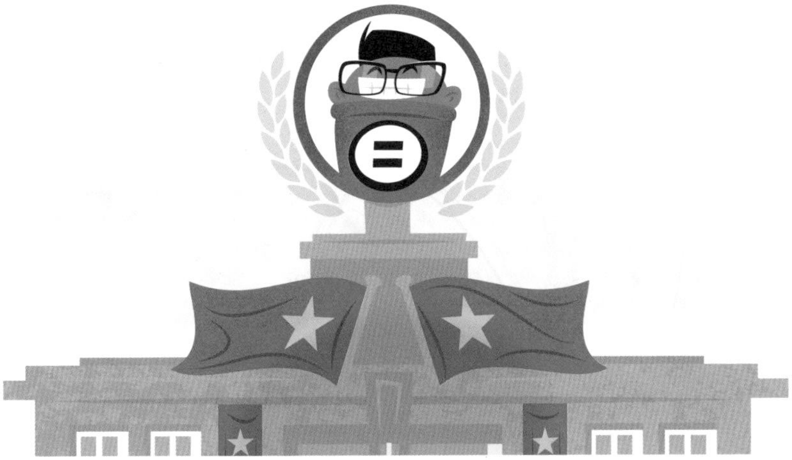

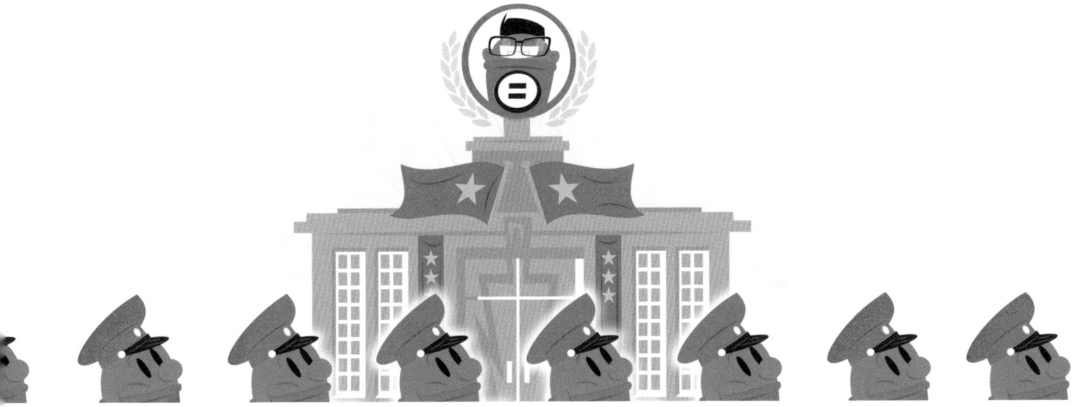

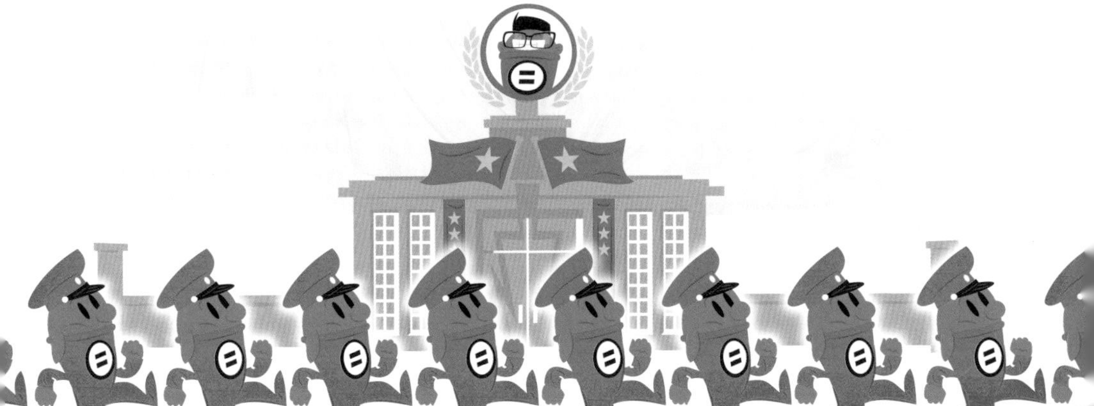

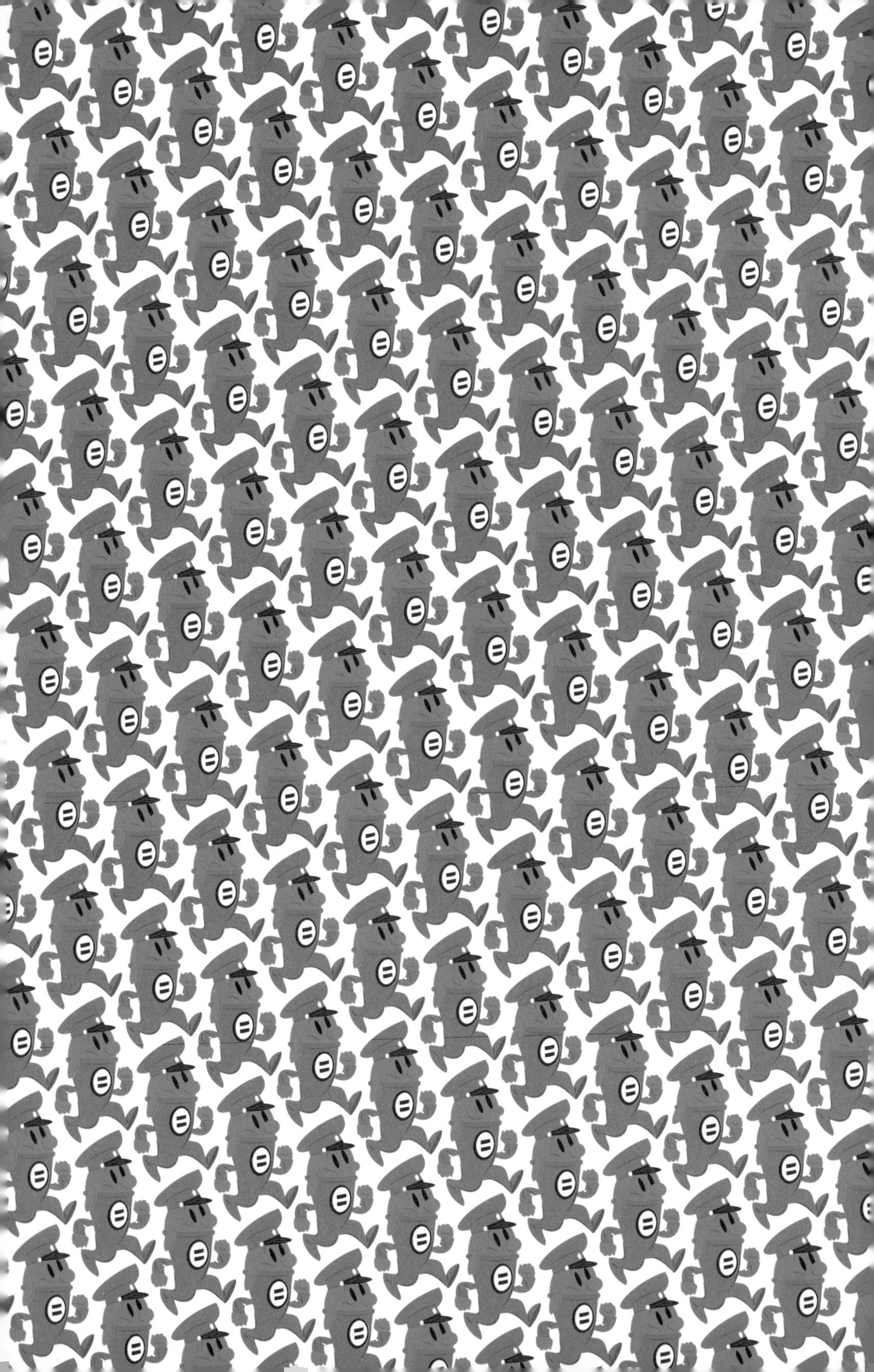

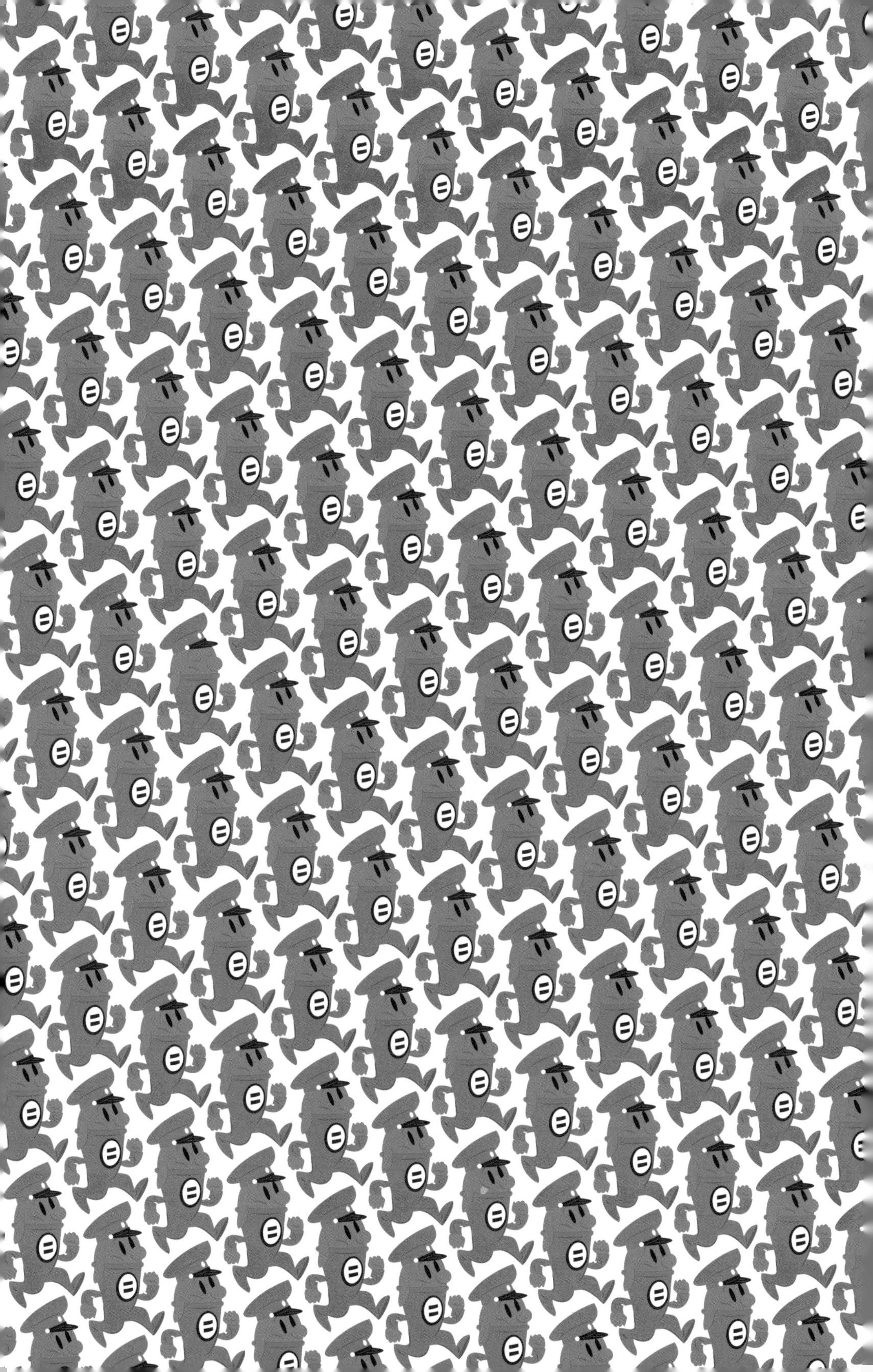

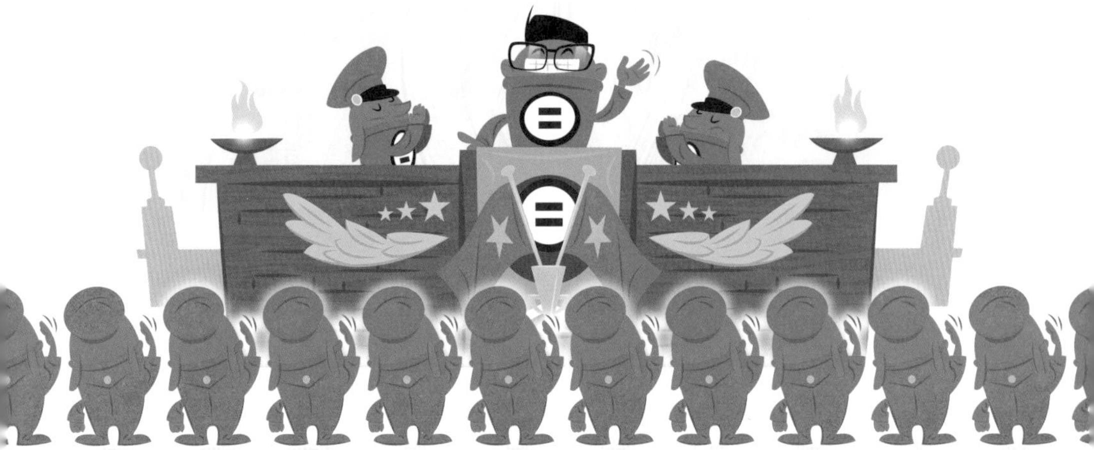

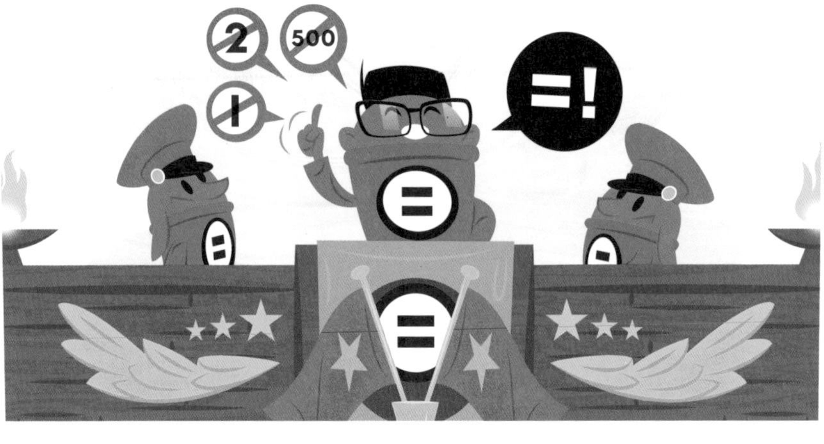
2
500
1
=!

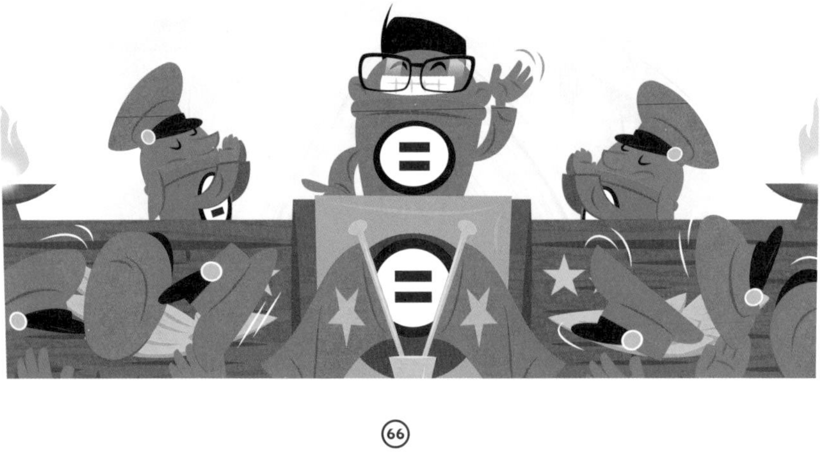

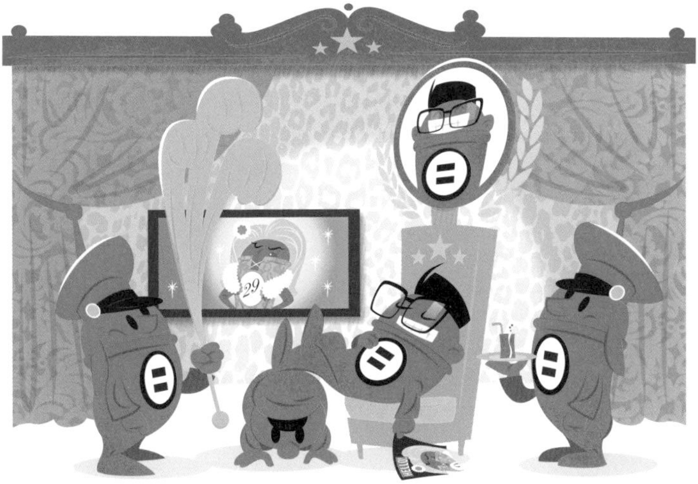
29
HELLO

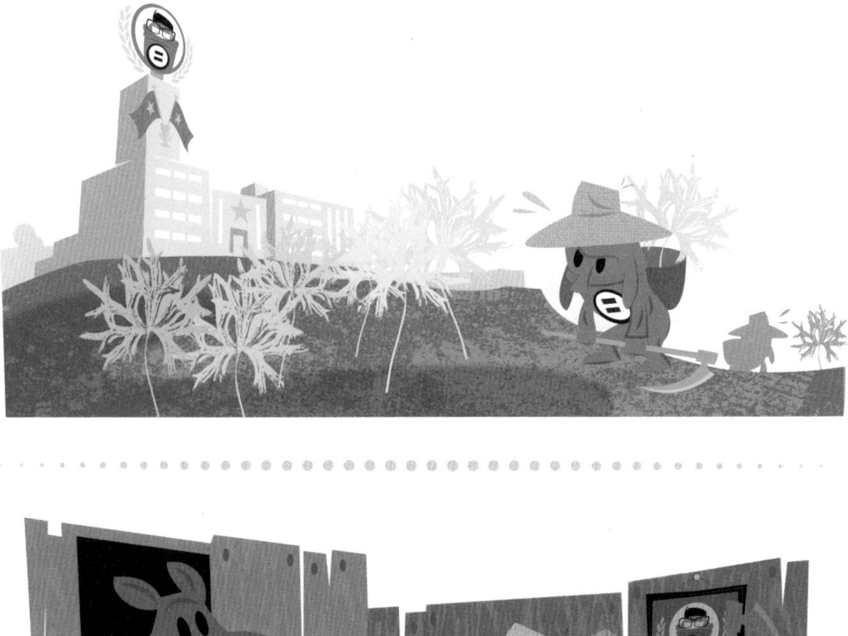

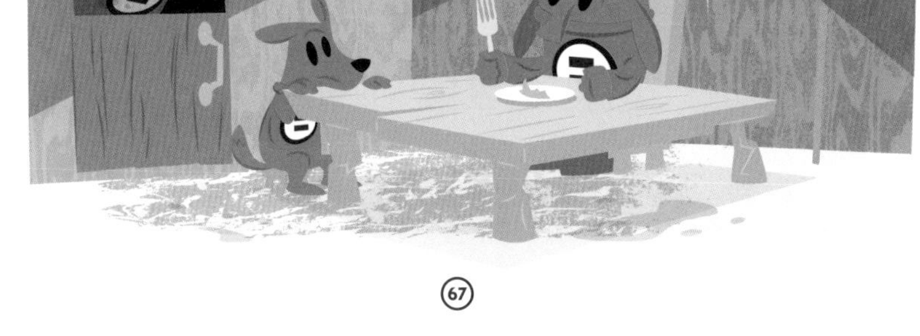

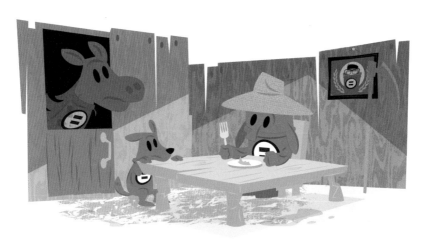

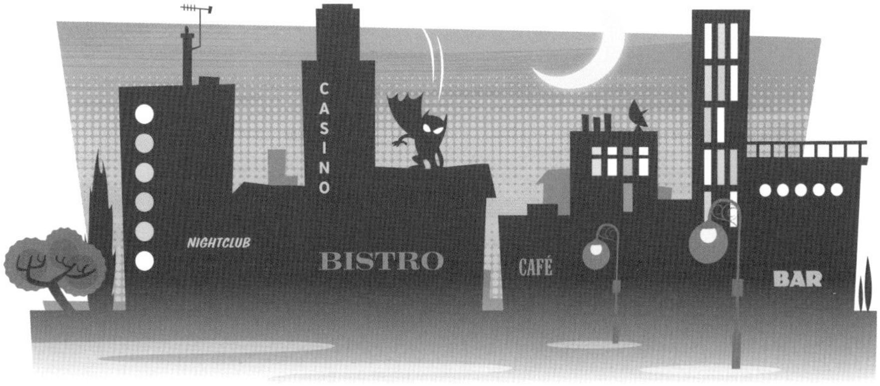
CASINO
NIGHTCLUB
BISTRO
CAFÉ
BAR

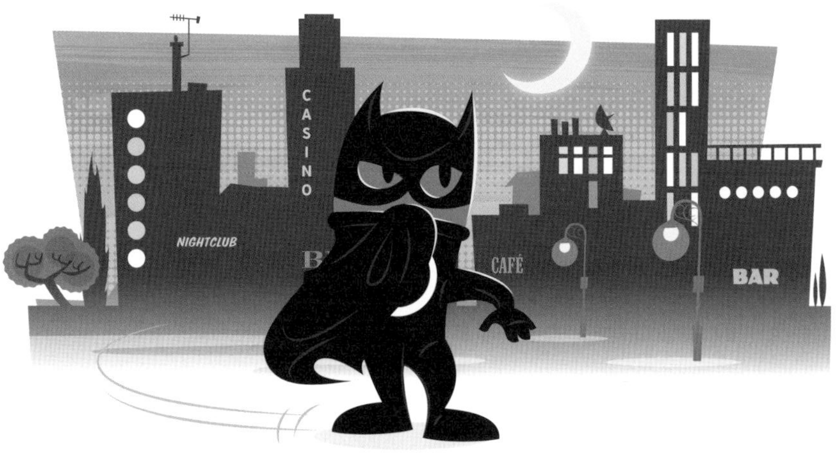
CASINO
NIGHTCLUB
CAFÉ
BAR

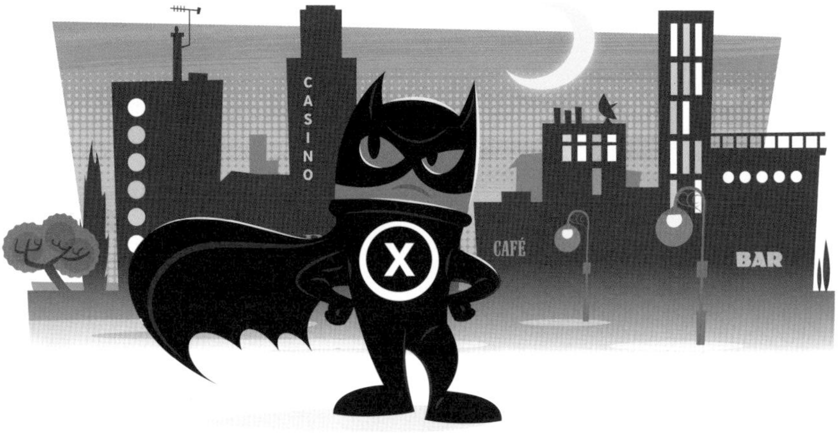
CASINO
CAFÉ
BAR
X

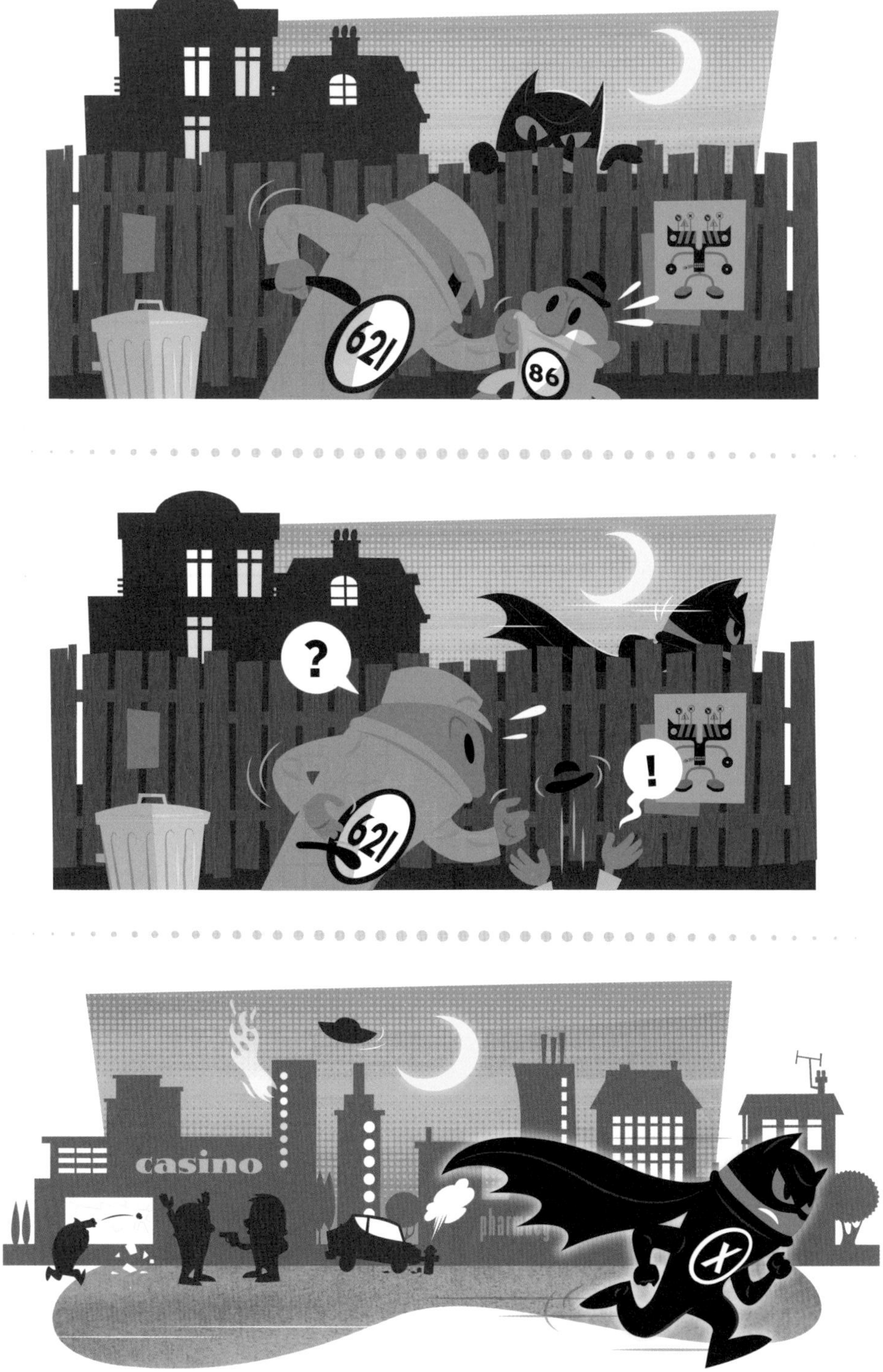
621
86
?
!
621
casino
X

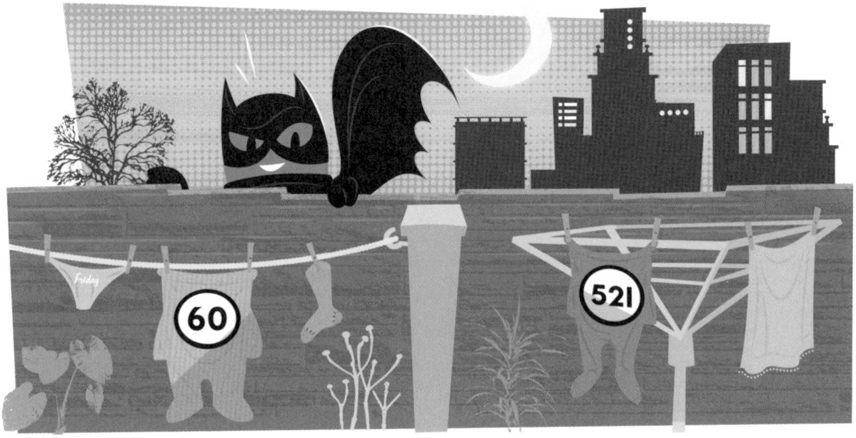
Friday
60
521

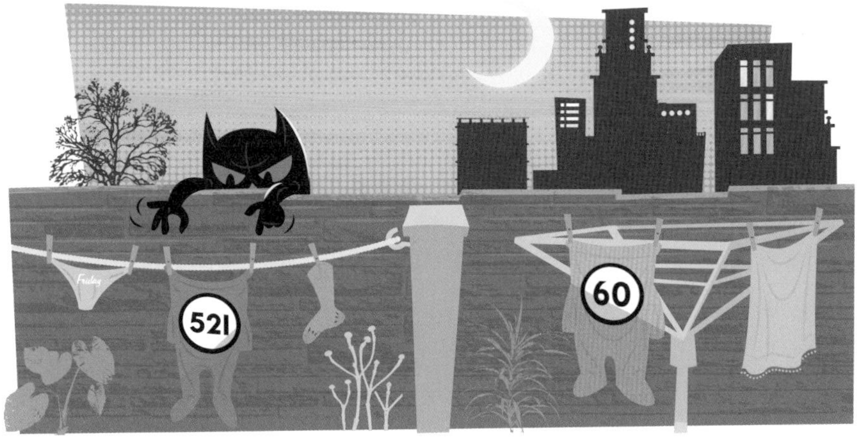
Friday
521
60

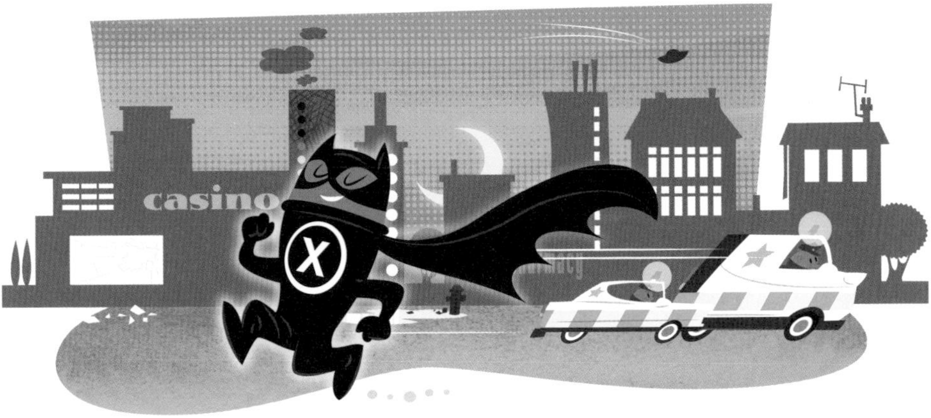
casino
X

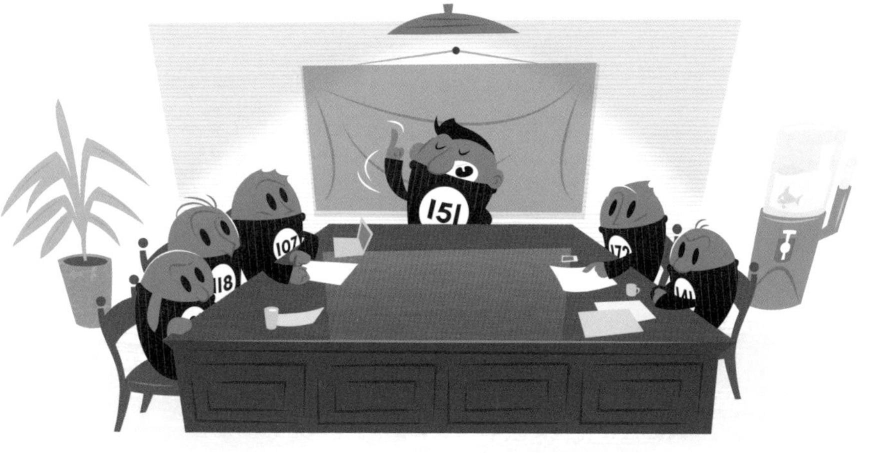
151
118

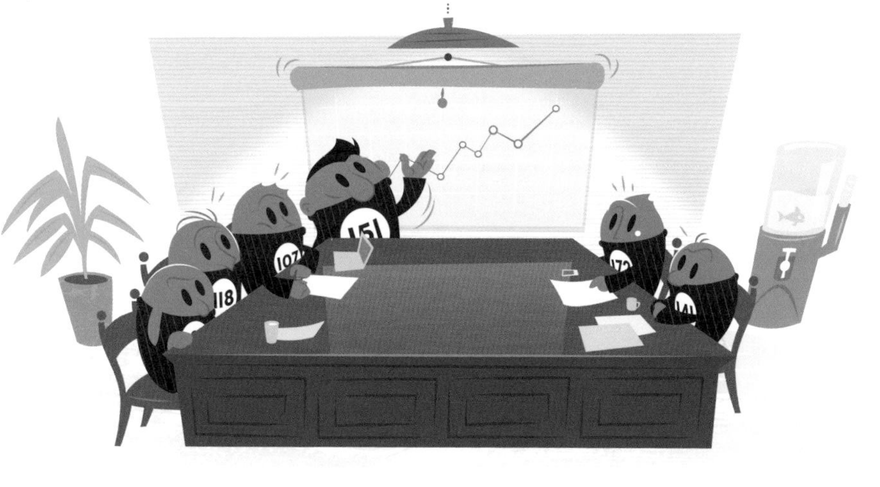
151
118
141

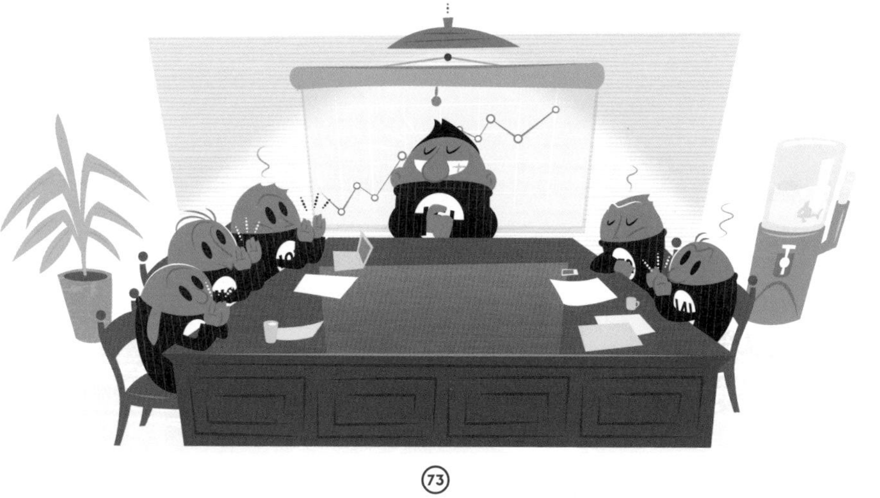
141

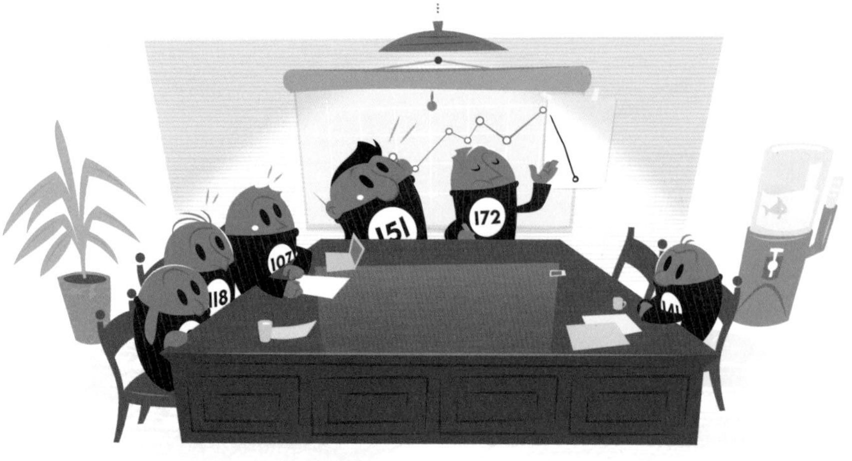
151
172
107
118
141

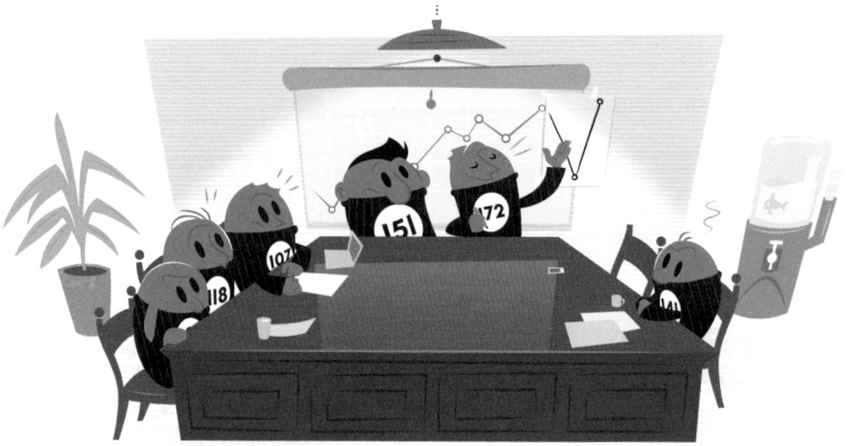
151
172
107
118
141

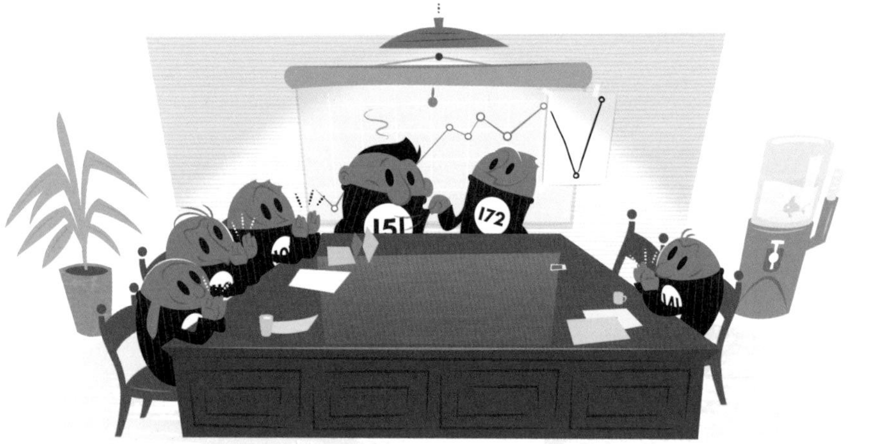
151
172
141

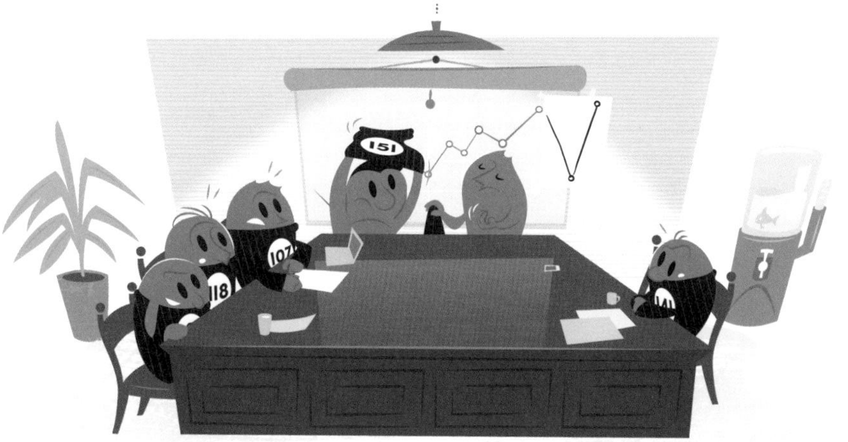
151
107
118
141

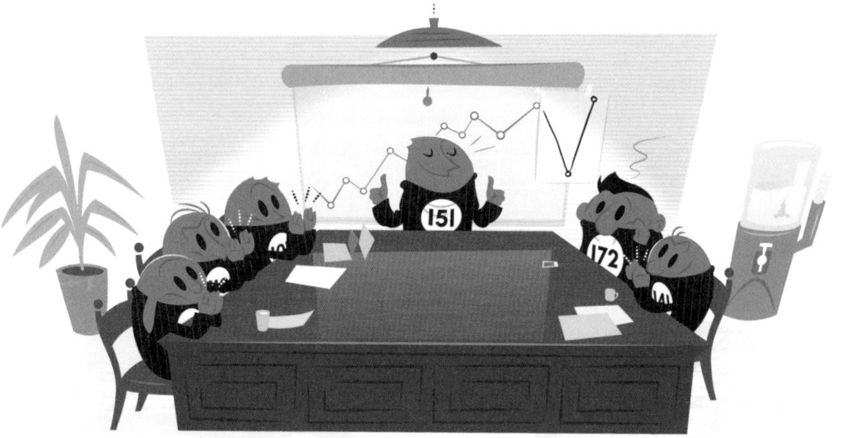
151
172
141

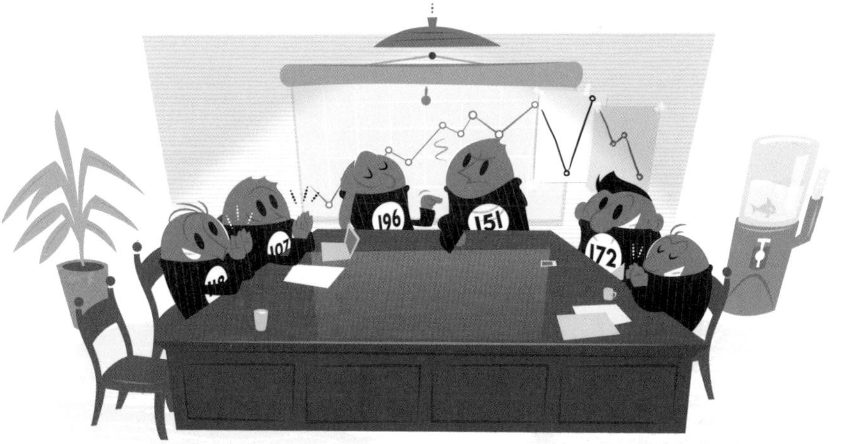
196
151
107
172

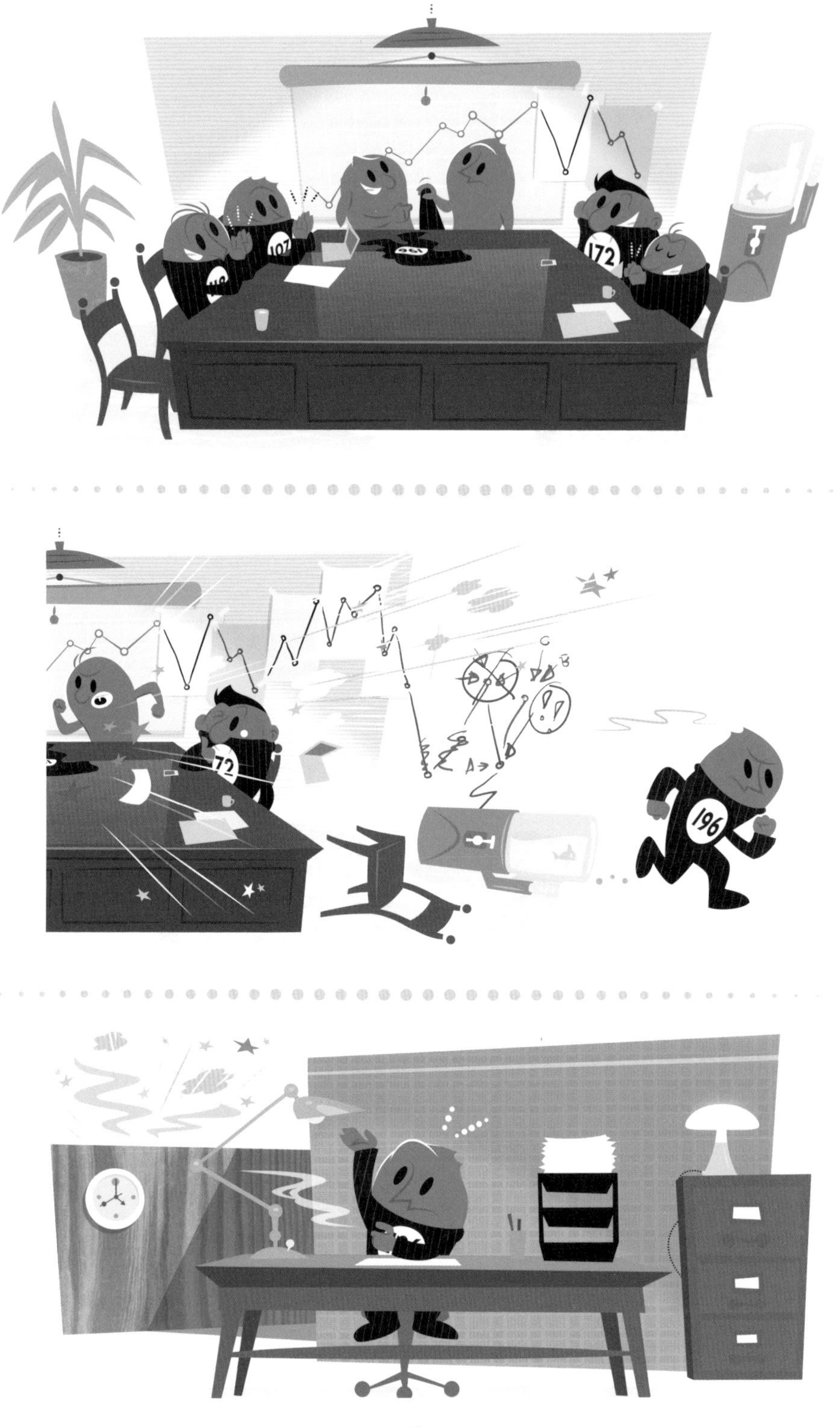
107
172
72
196

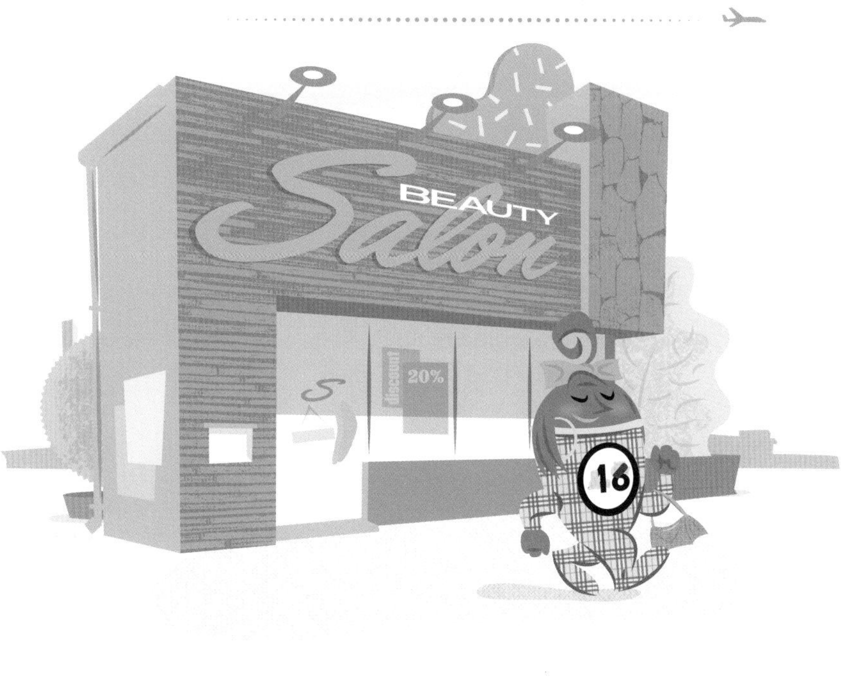
BEAUTY
Salon
discount
20%
16

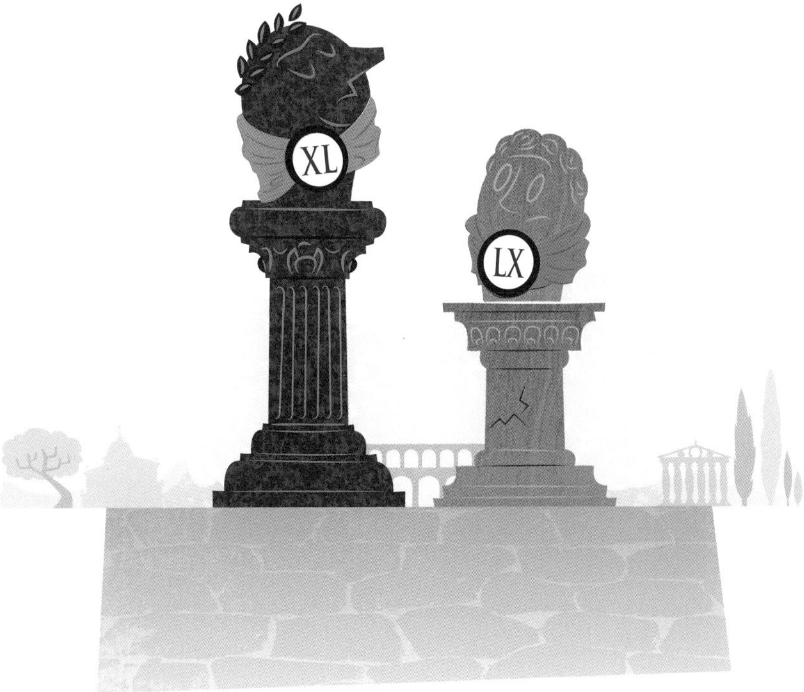
XL
LX

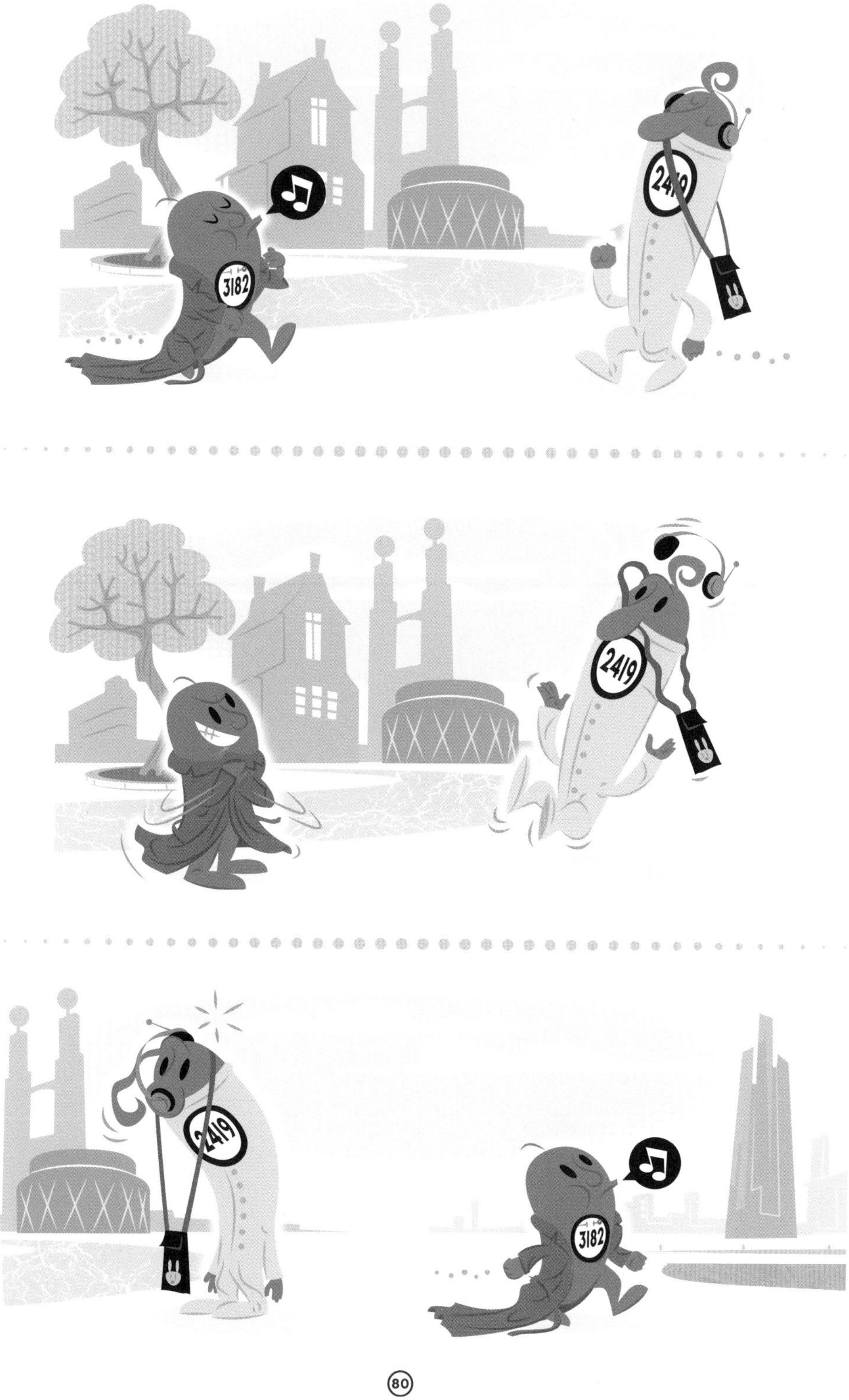
3182
2419
2419
2419
3182

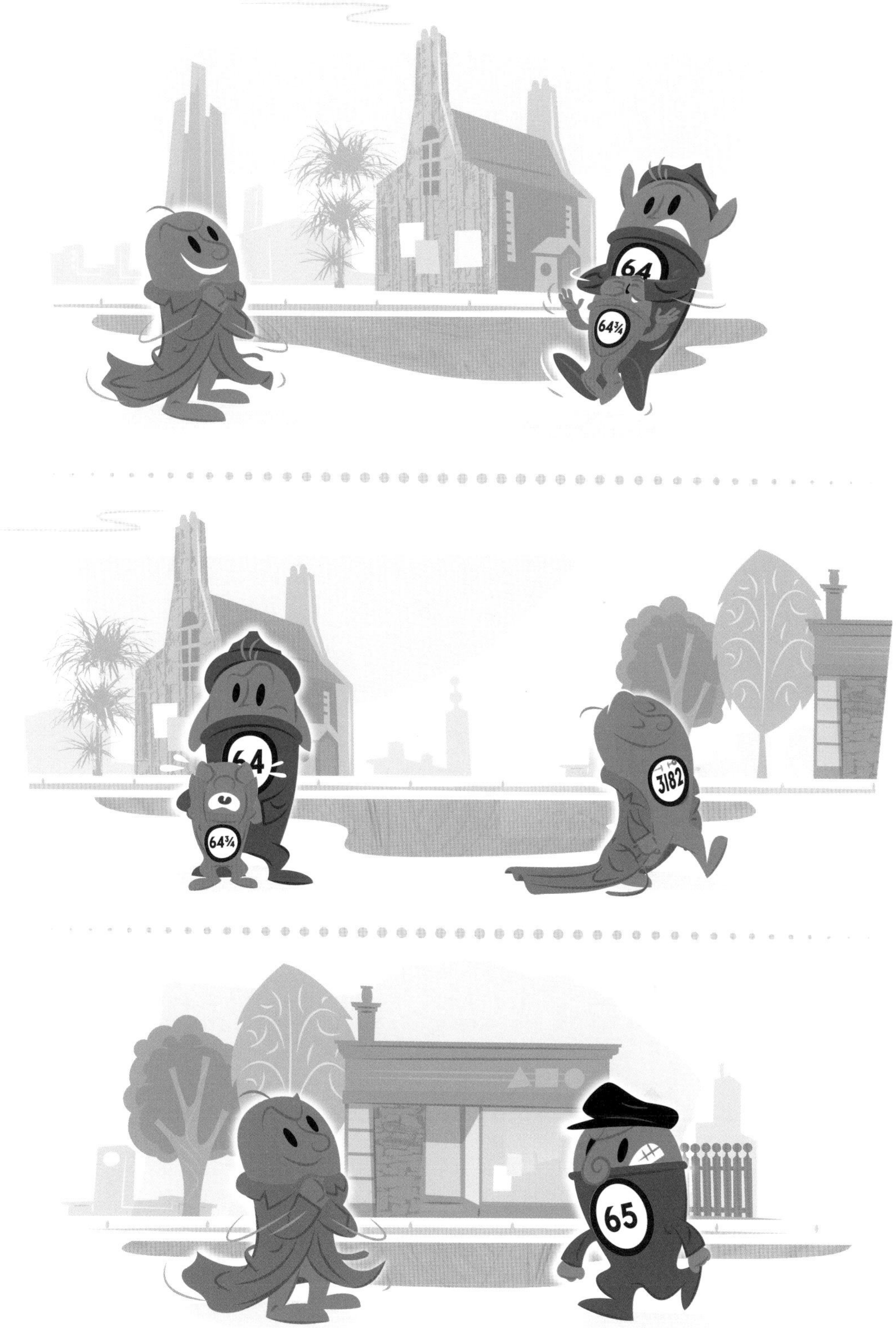
64
64¾
64
64¾
3182
65

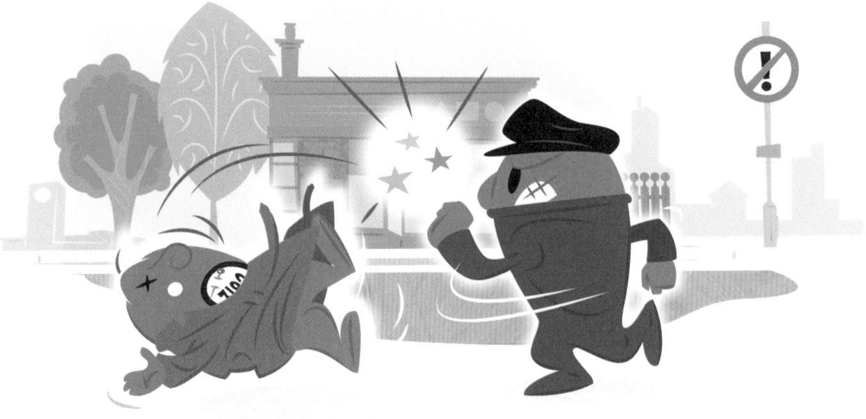

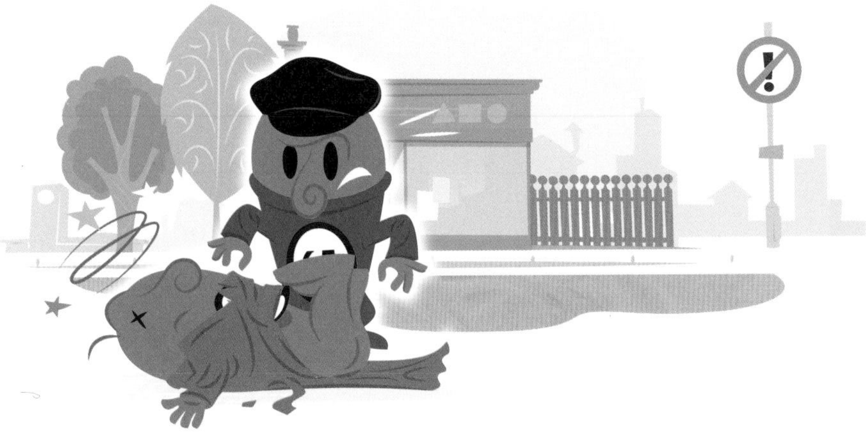

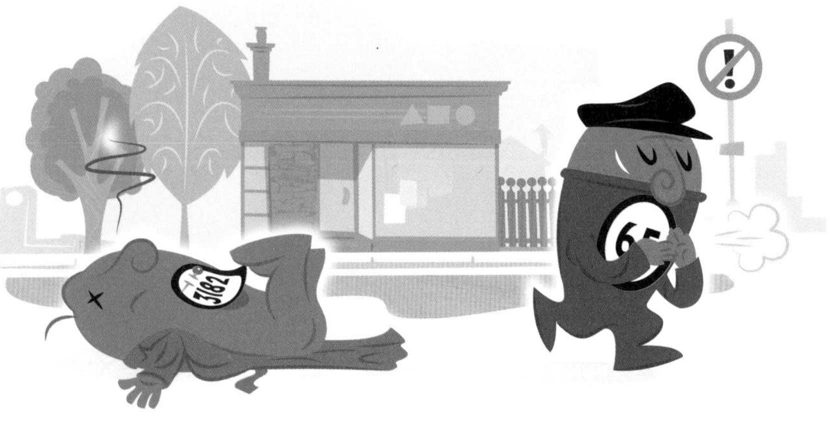
3182
65

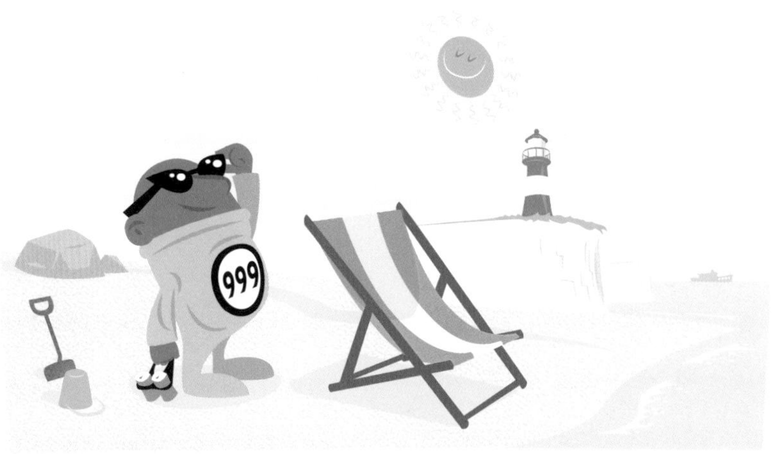
999

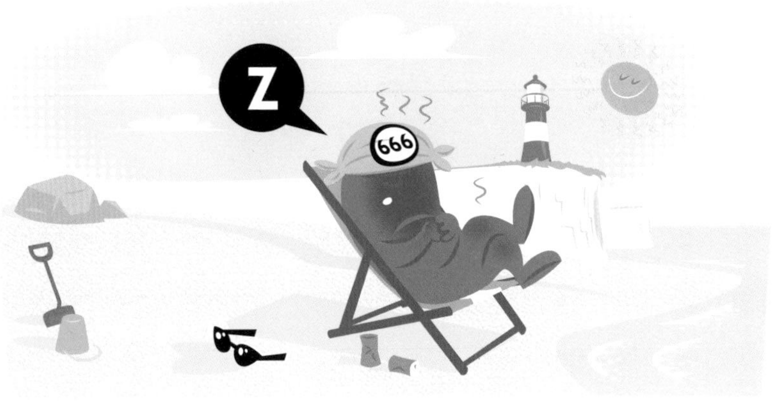
Z
666

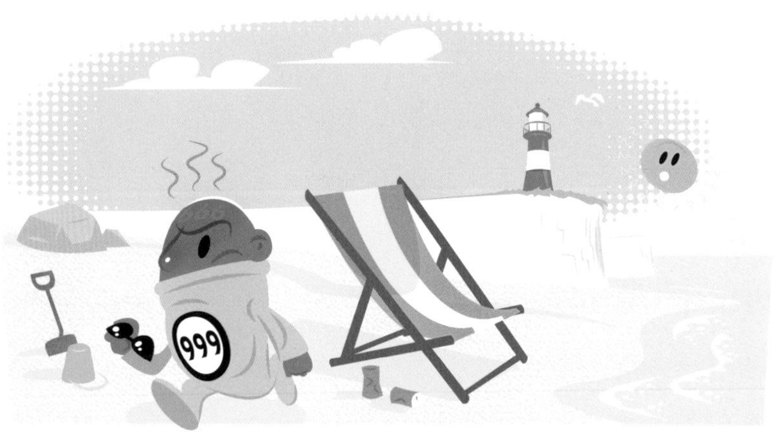
999

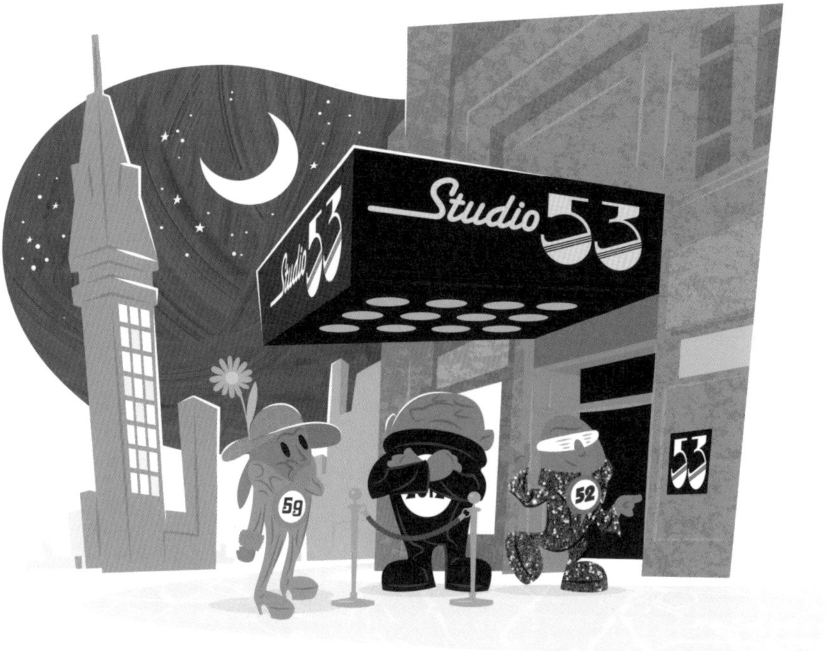
Studio 53
Studio 53
53
59
52

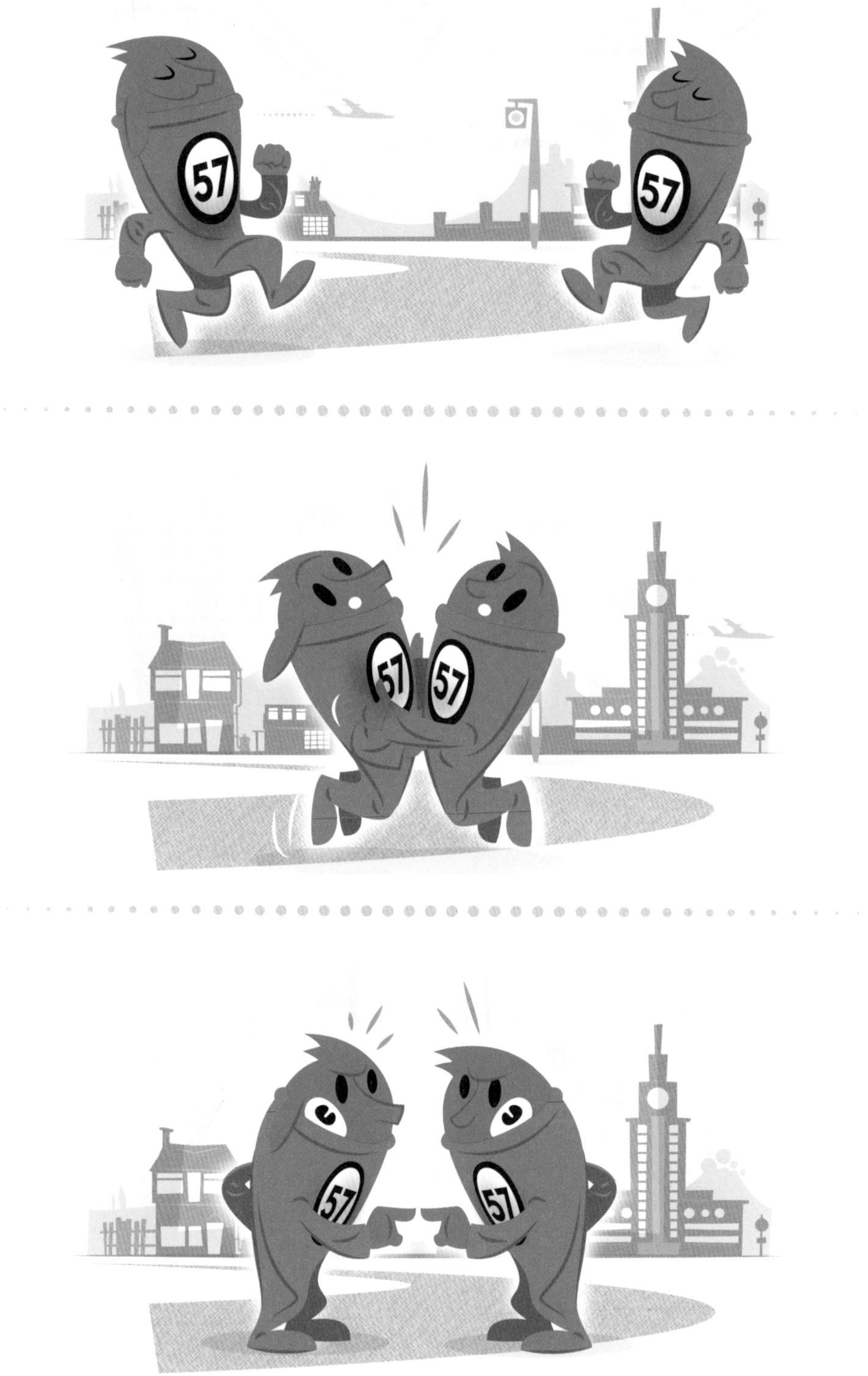
57
57
57
57
57
57

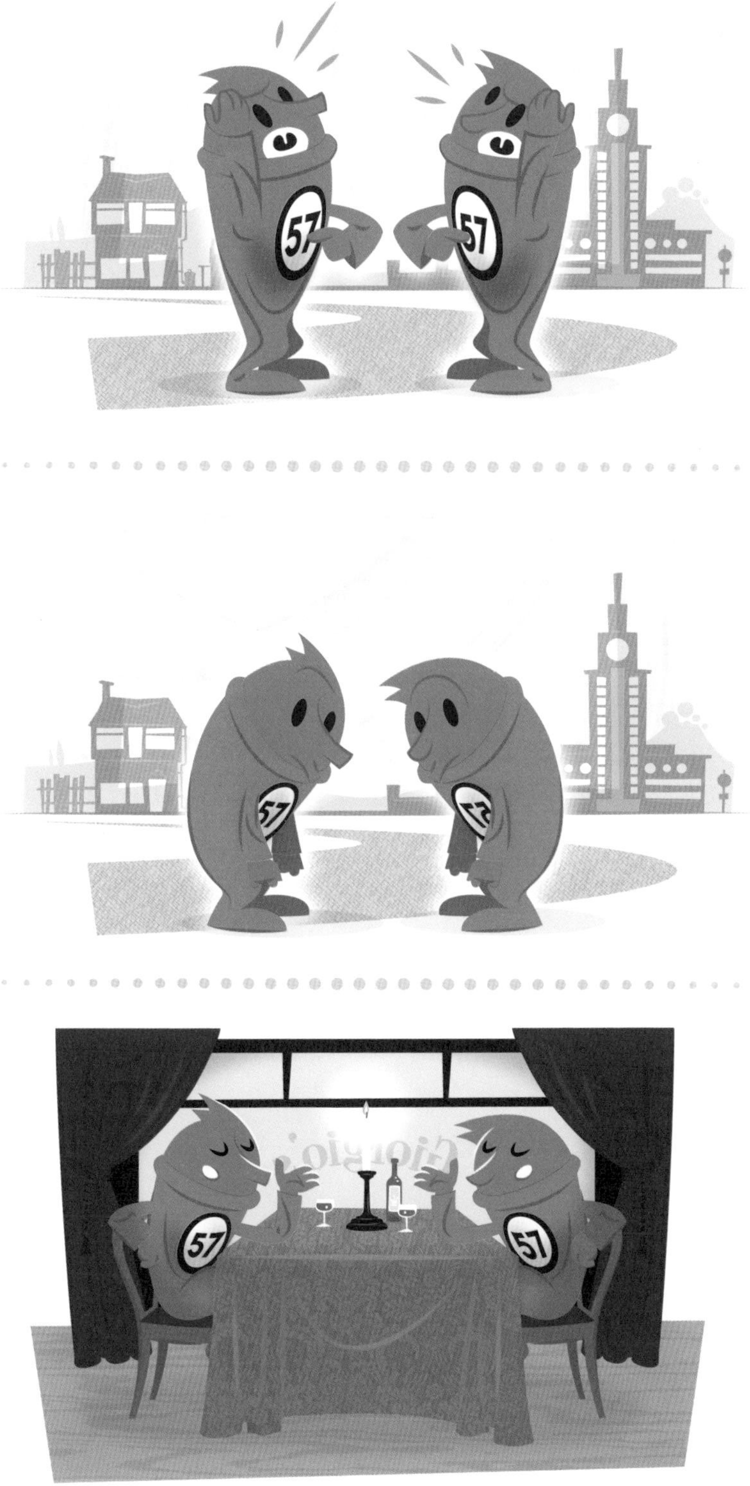
57
57
57
57

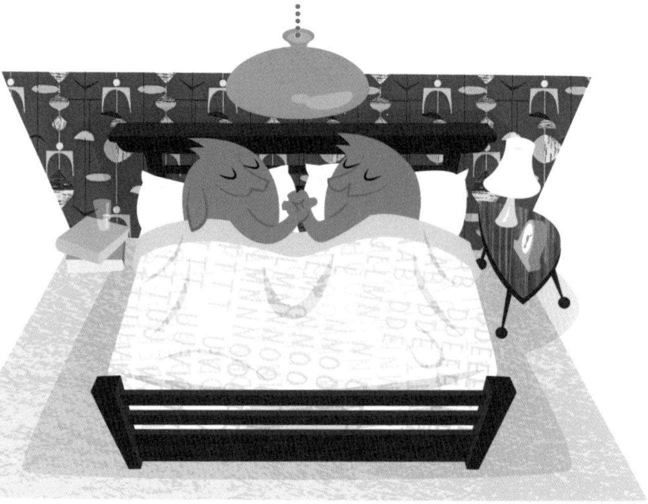

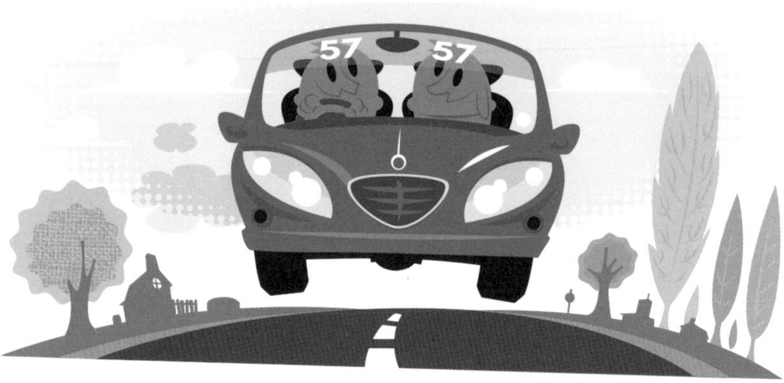
57
57

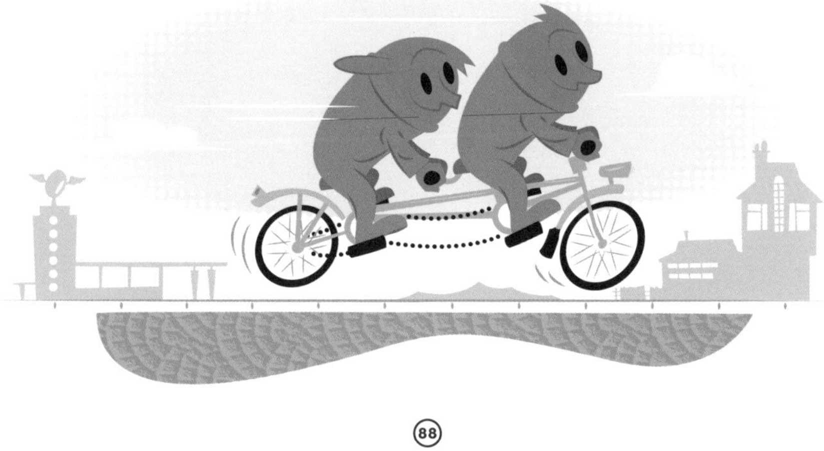

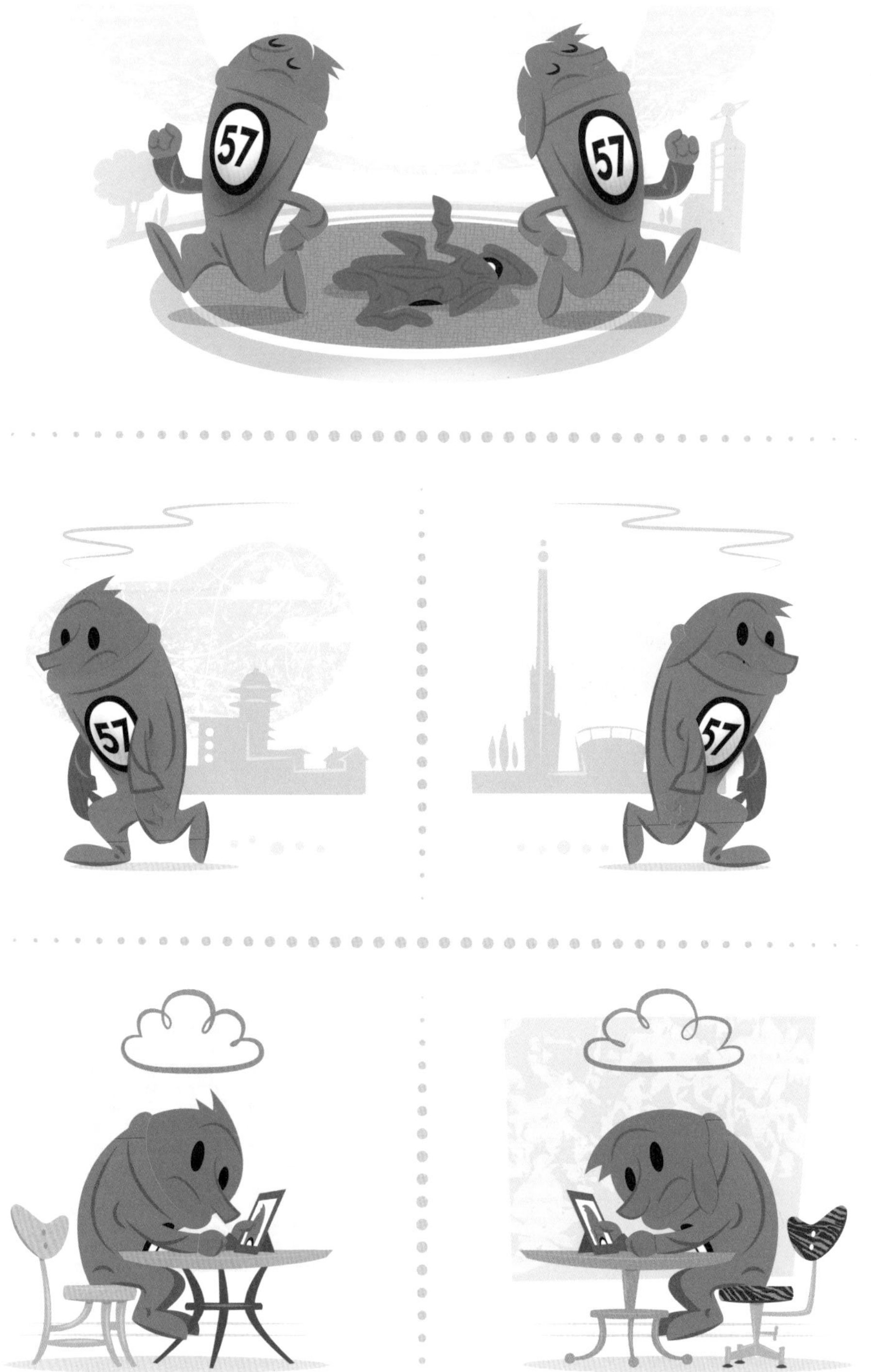
57
57
57
57

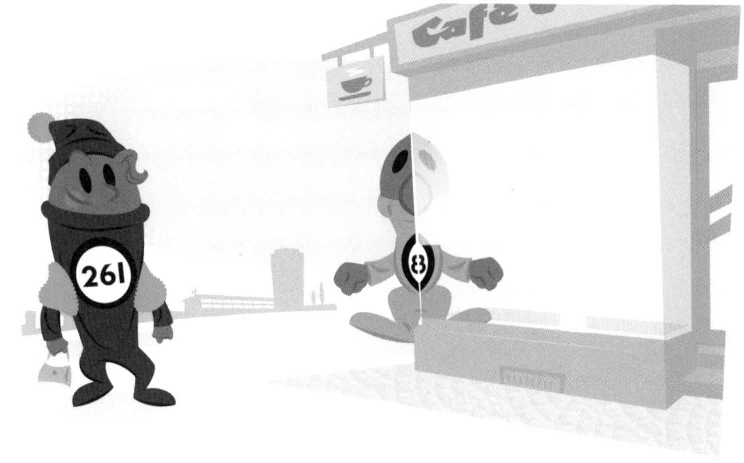
Café
261

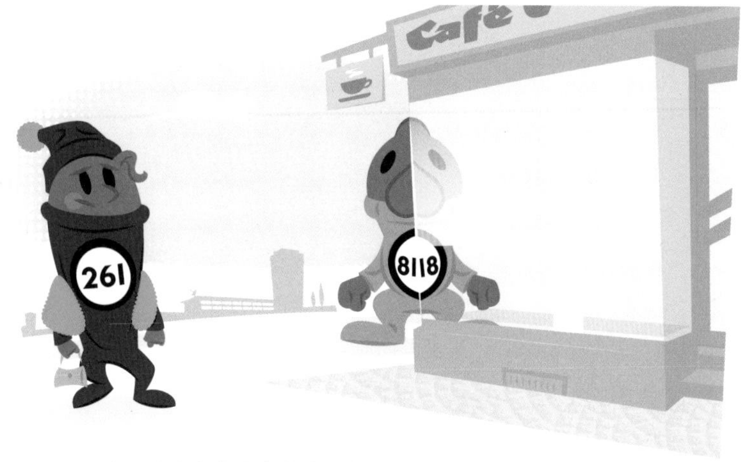
Café
261
8118

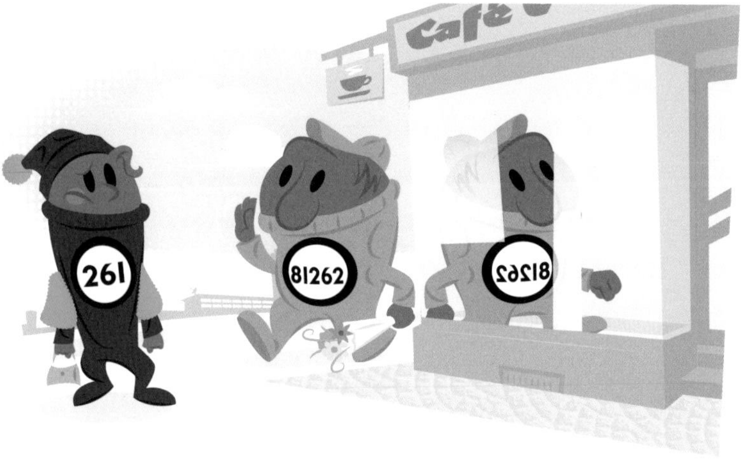
Café
261
81262

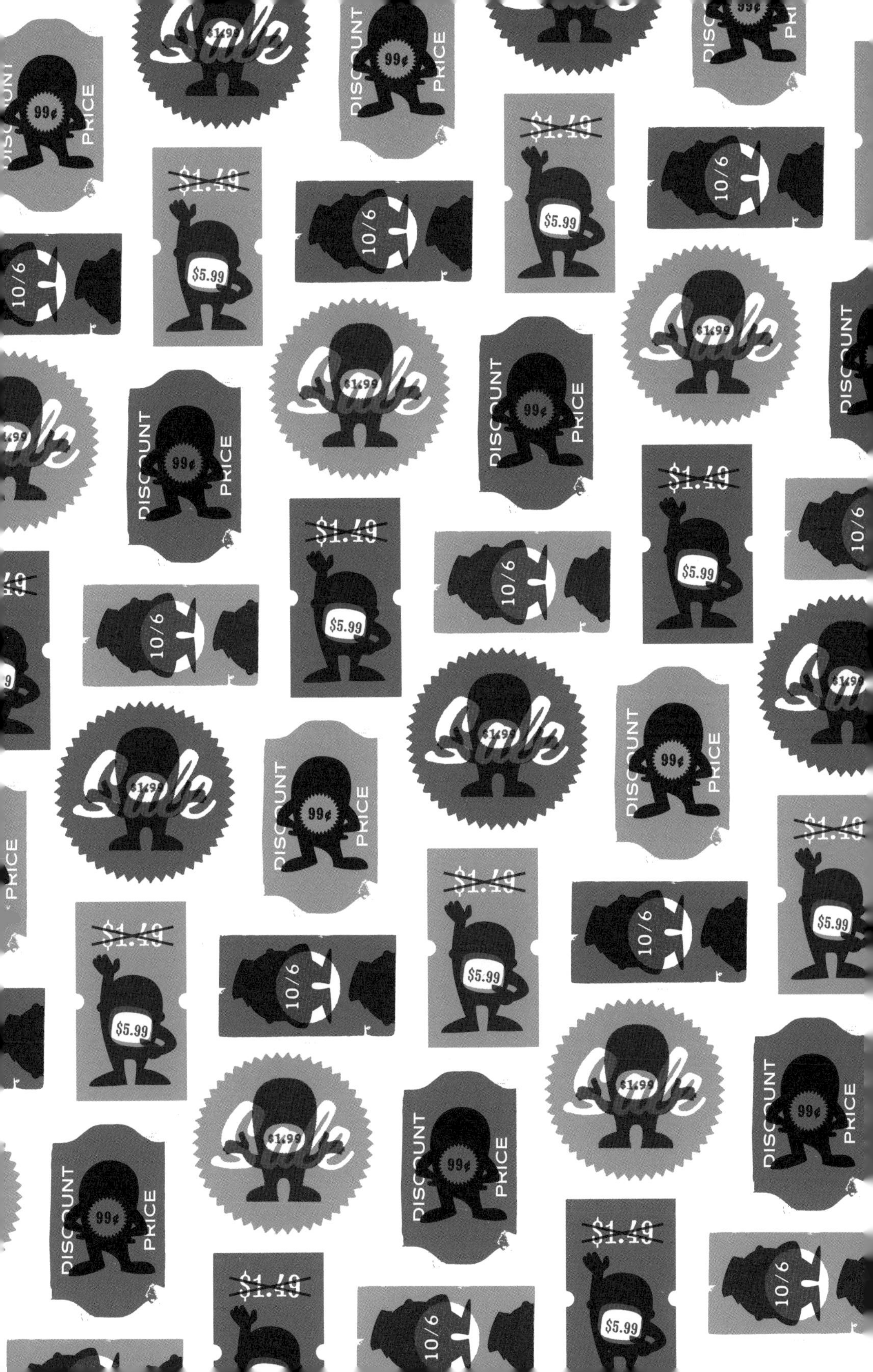
DISCOUNT PRICE
99¢
Sale
$14.99
$1.49
$5.99
10/6

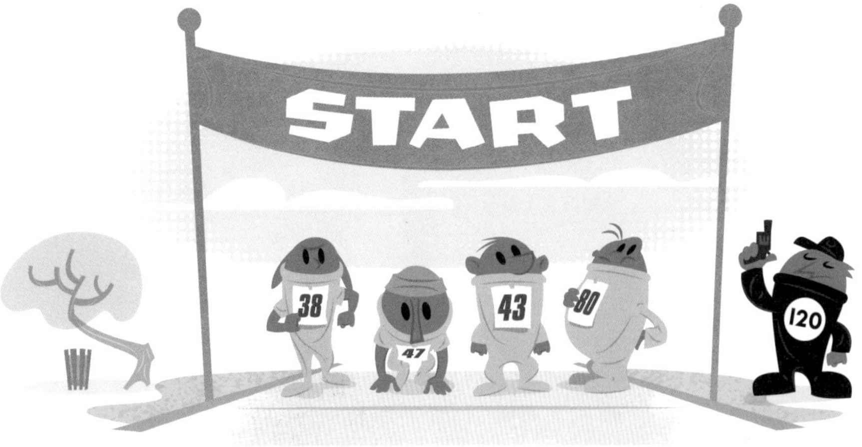
START
38
47
43
80
120

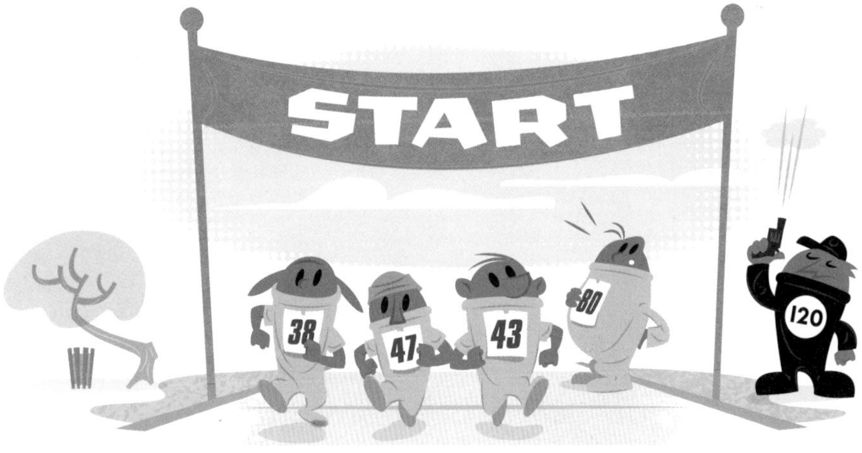
START
38
47
43
80
120

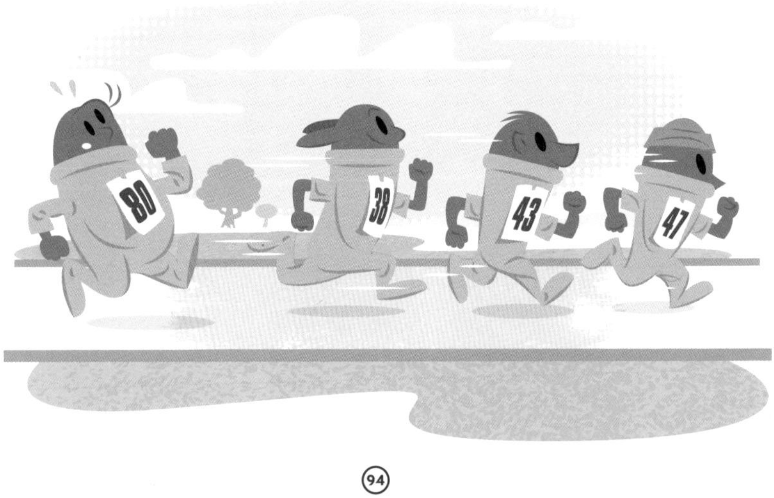
80
38
43
47

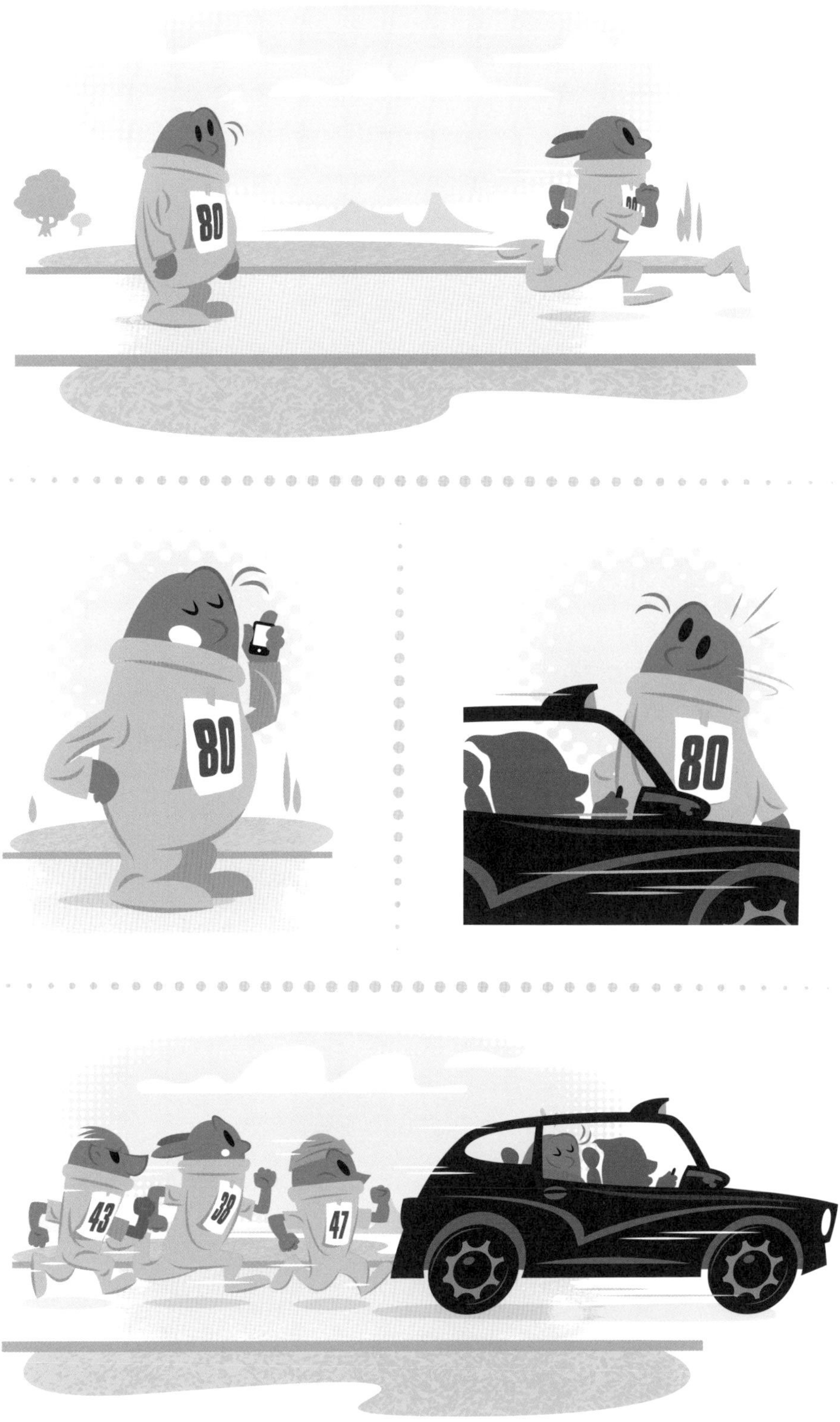
80
80
80
43
38
47

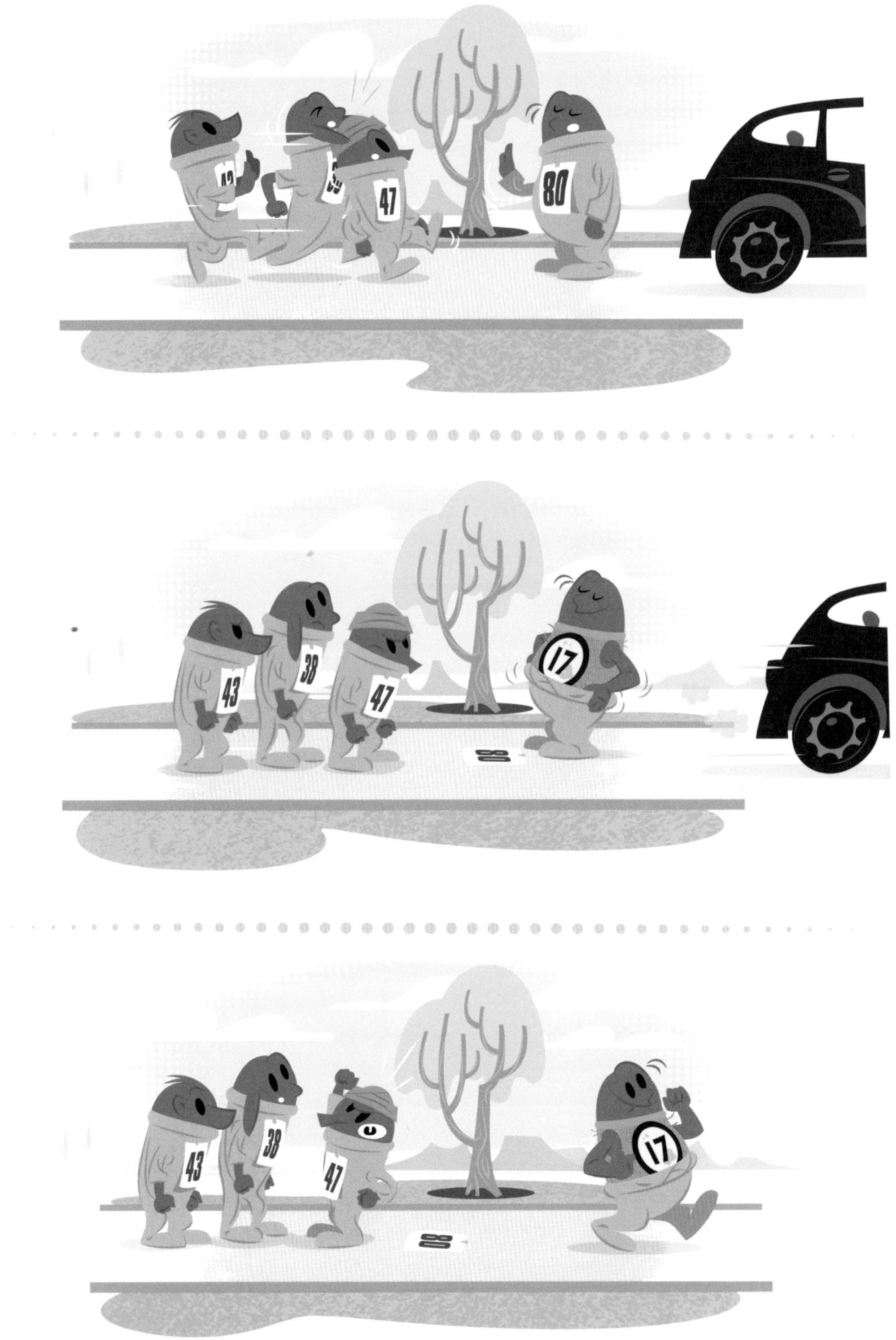
47
80
43
38
47
17
43
38
47
17

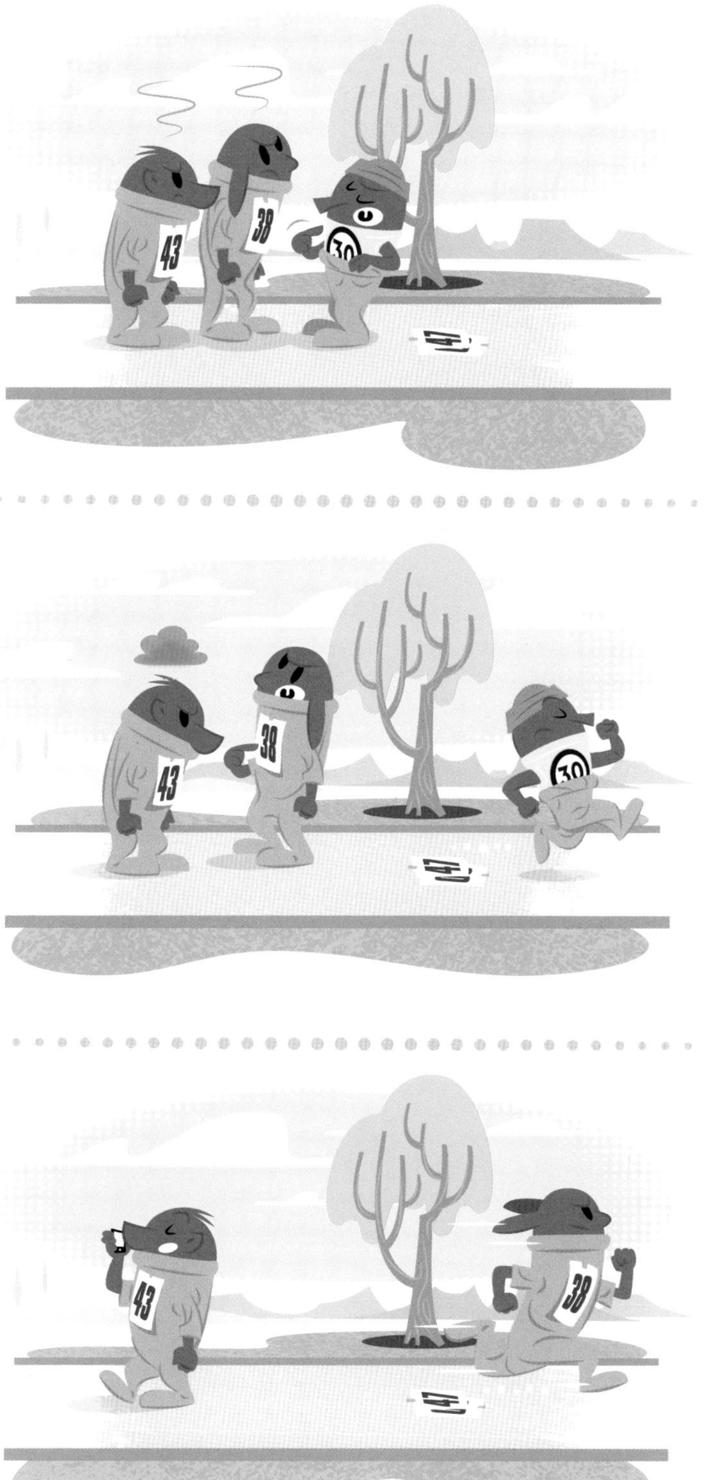
43
38
30
43
38
30
43
38

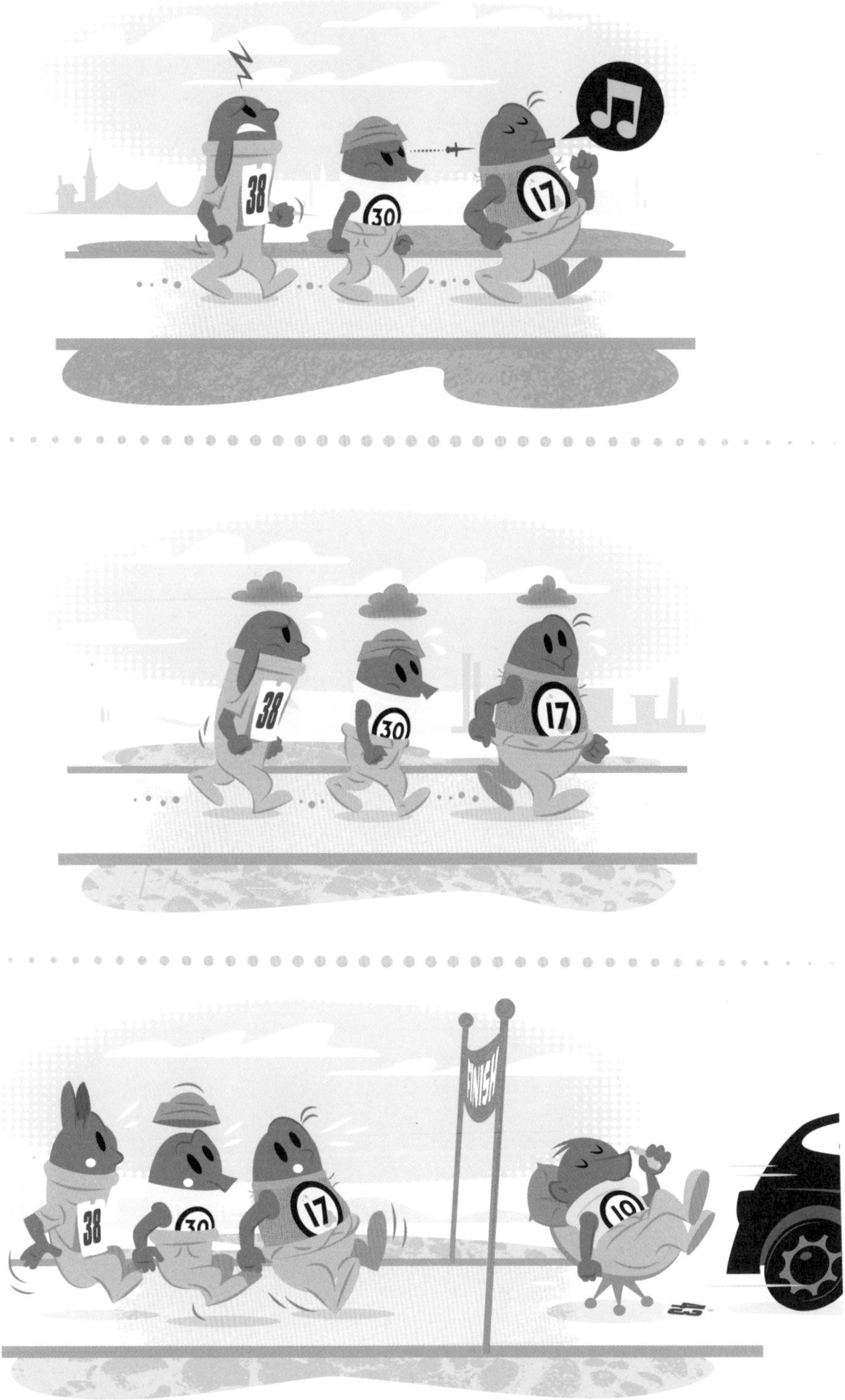
38
30
17
38
30
17
38
30
17
FINISH
10

ISBN 978-1-60309-419-1
I AM A NUMBER
ISBN 978-1-60309-419-1
I AM A NUMBER
ISBN 978-1-60309-419-1
I AM A NUMBER
ISBN 978-1-60309-419-1
I AM A NUMBER
ISBN 978-1-60309-419-1
I AM A NUMBER
ISBN 978-1-60309-419-1
I AM A NUMBER
ISBN 978-1-60309-419-1
I AM A NUMBER
ISBN 978-1-60309-419-1
I AM A NUMBER
ISBN 978-1-60309-419-1
I AM A NUMBER

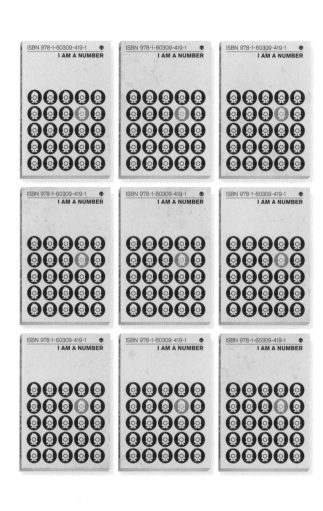

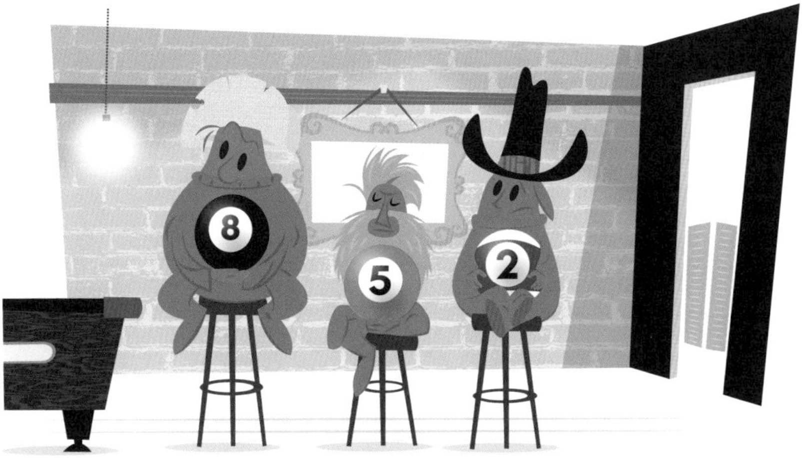
8
5
2

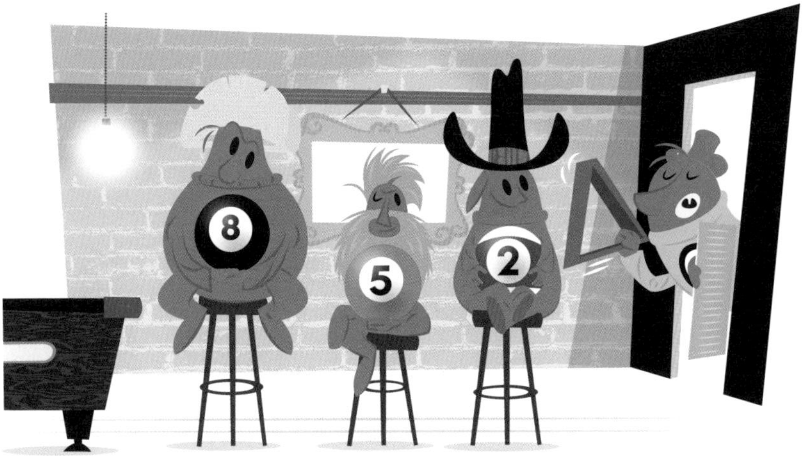
8
5
2

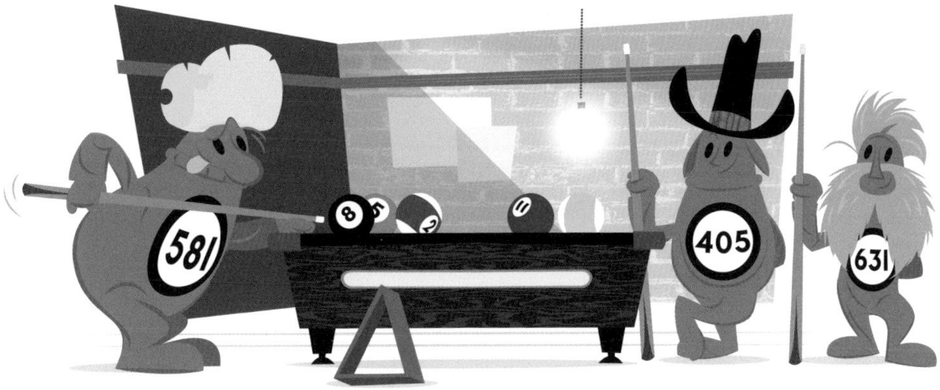
581
405
631

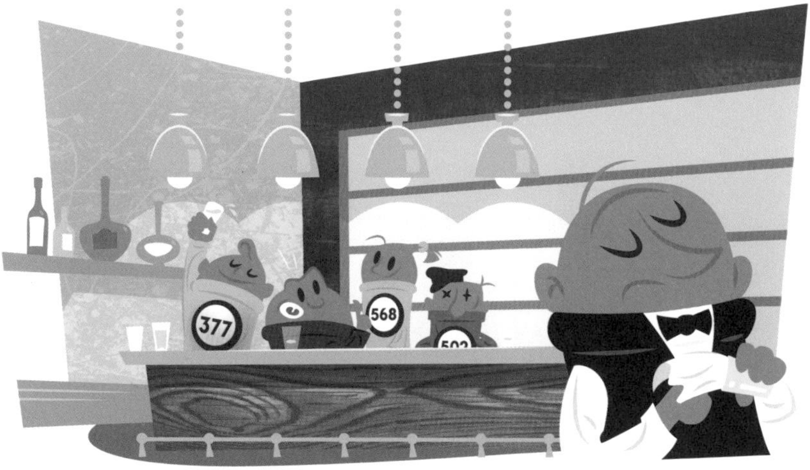
377
568

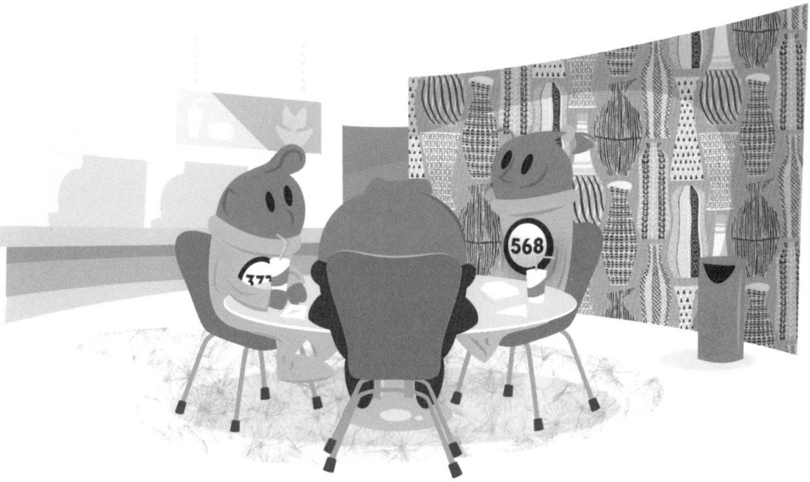
568

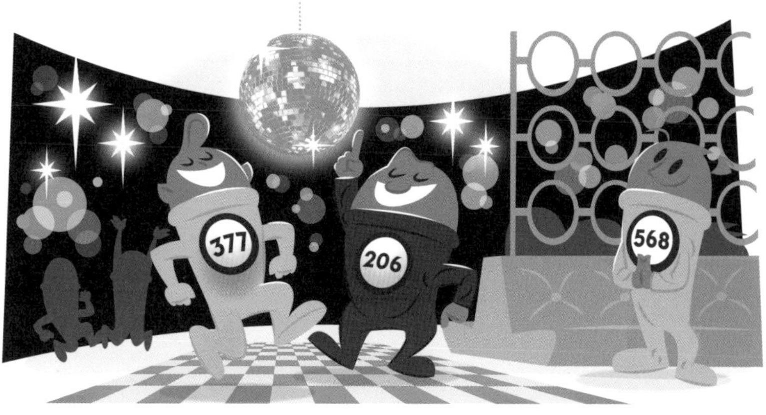
377
206
568

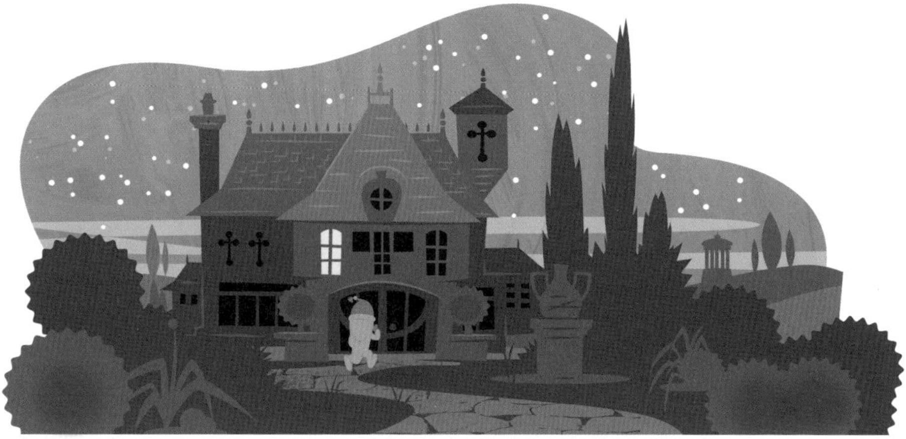

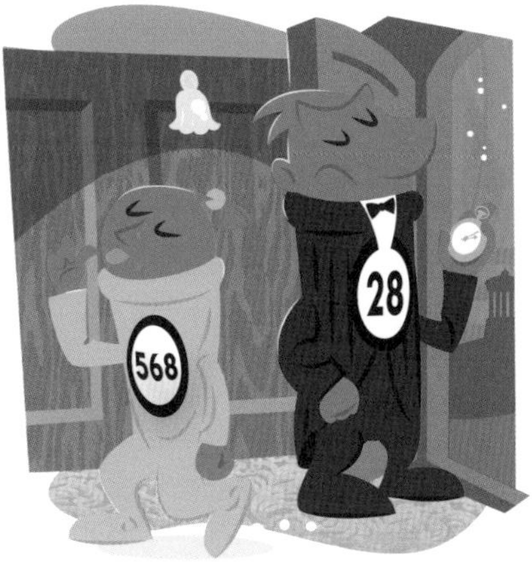
568
28

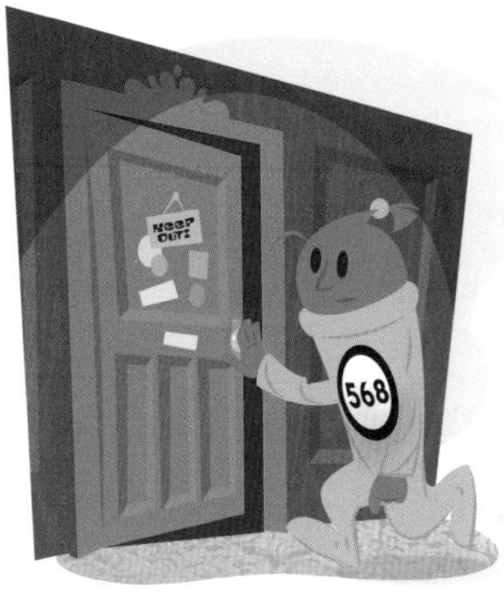
KEEP OUT!
568

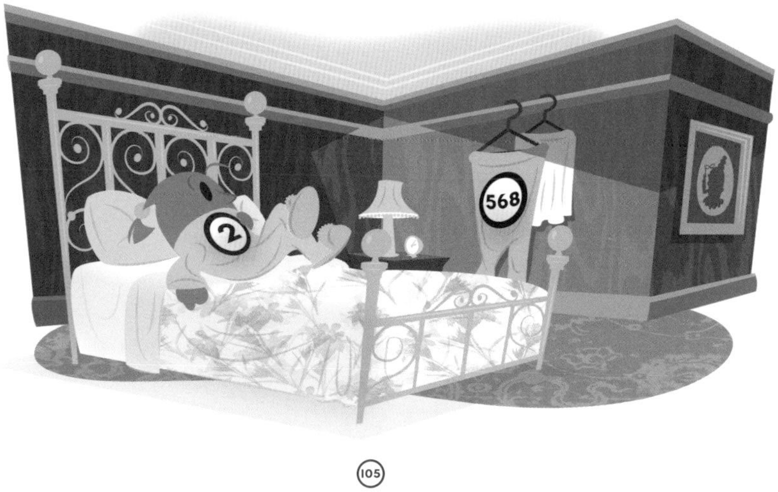
2
568

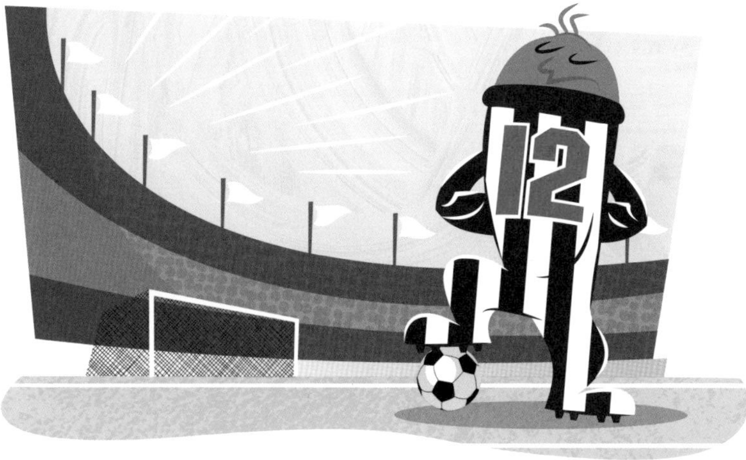
12

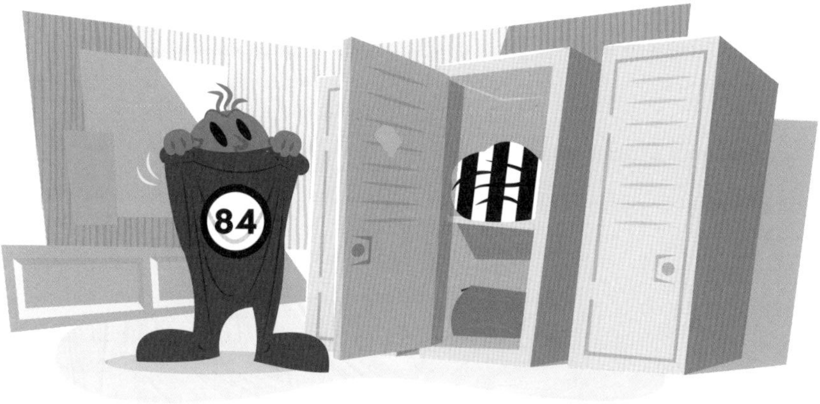
84

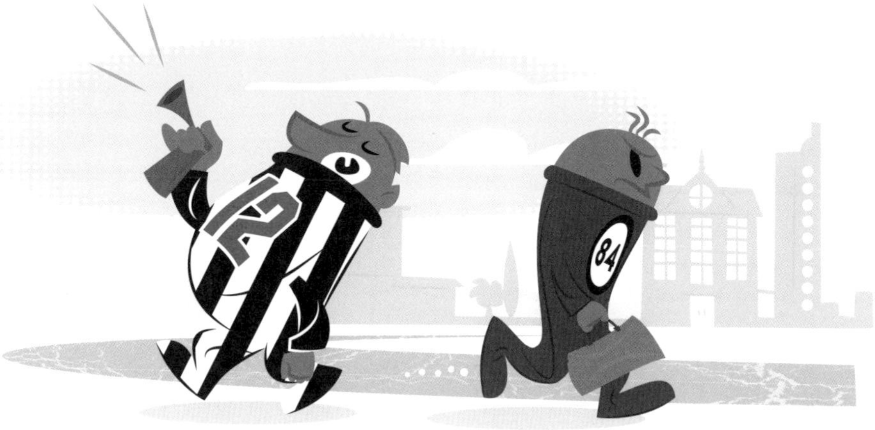
12
84

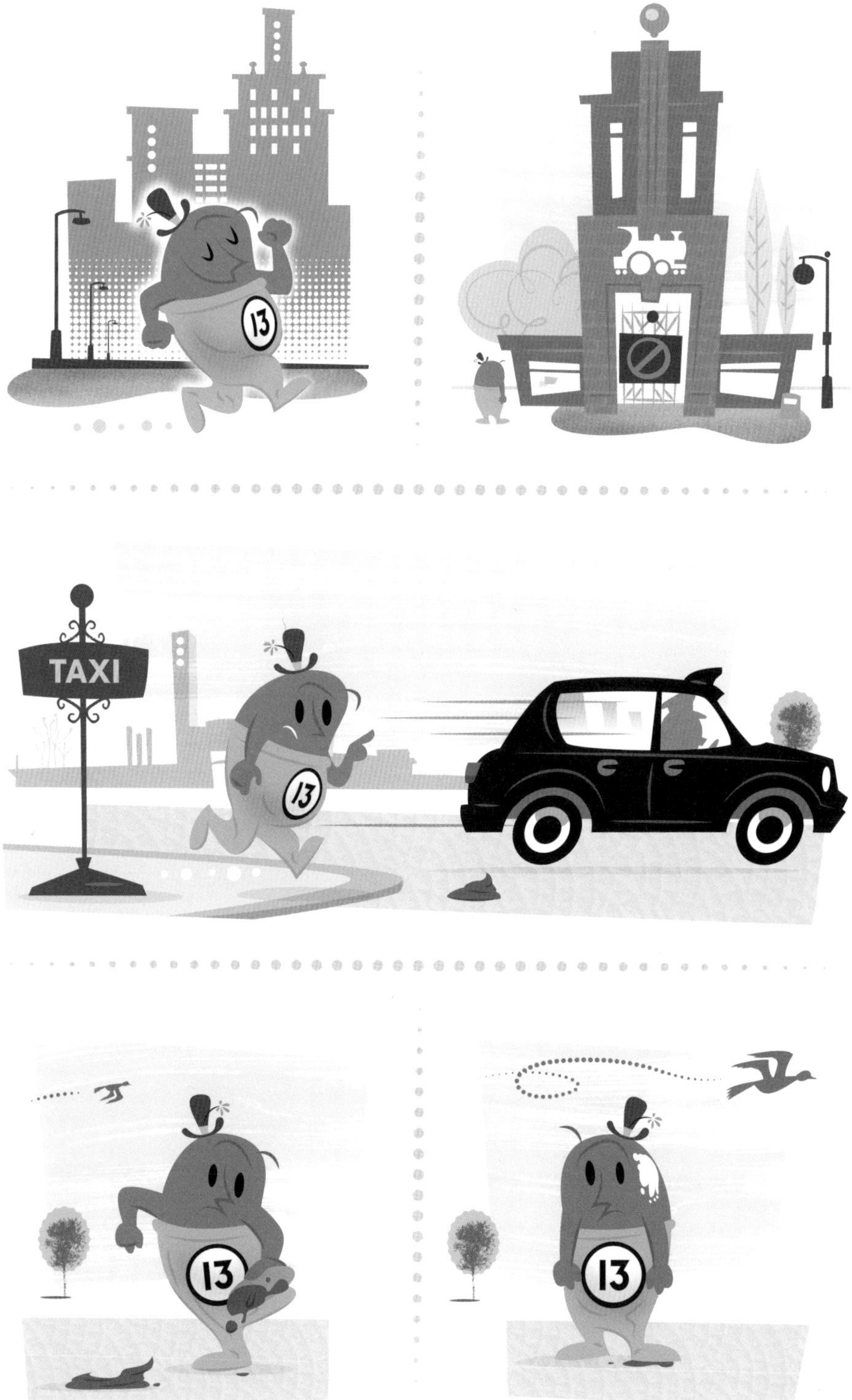
13
TAXI
13
13
13

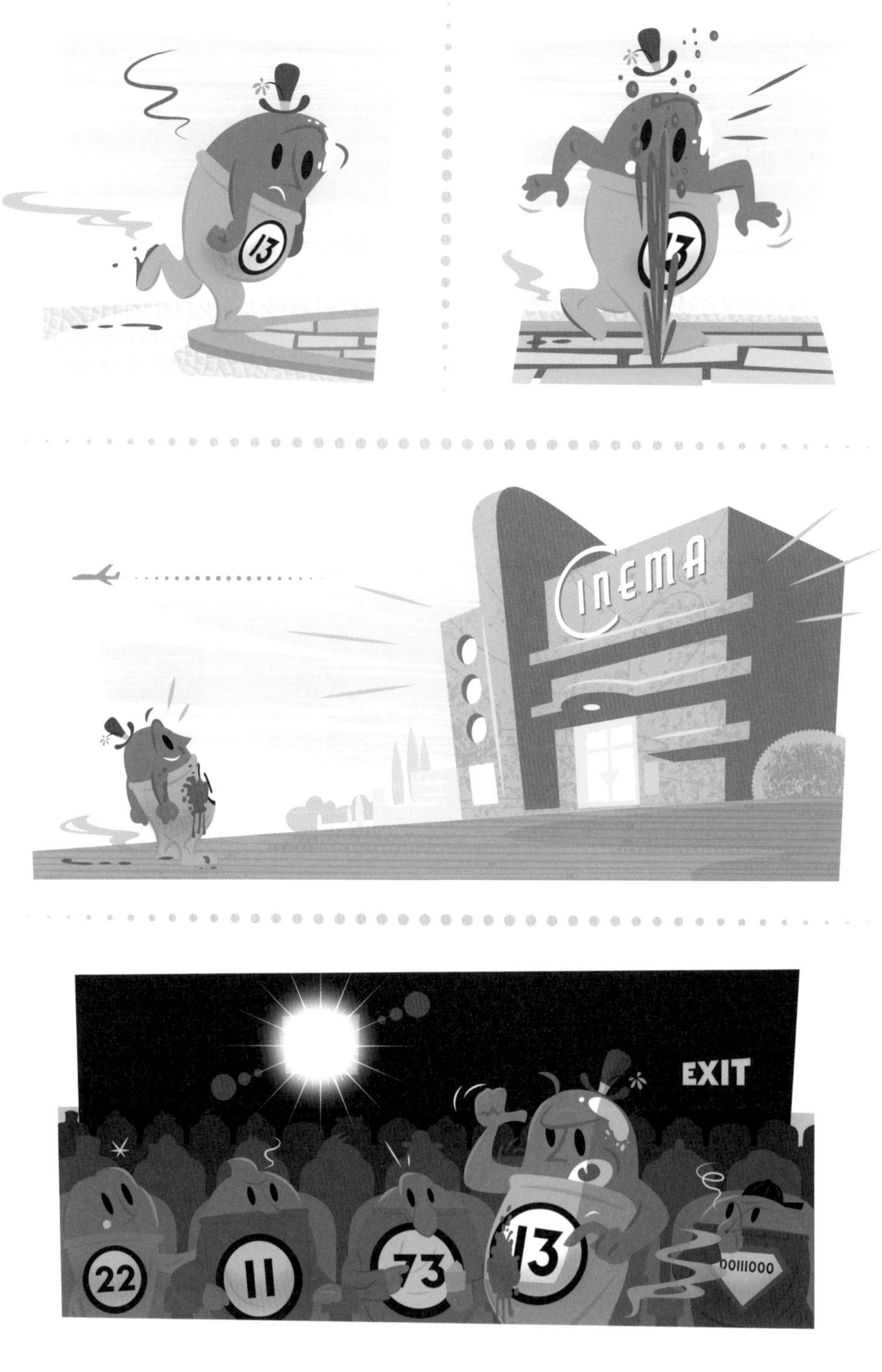
13
CINEMA
EXIT
22
11
73
13
00111000

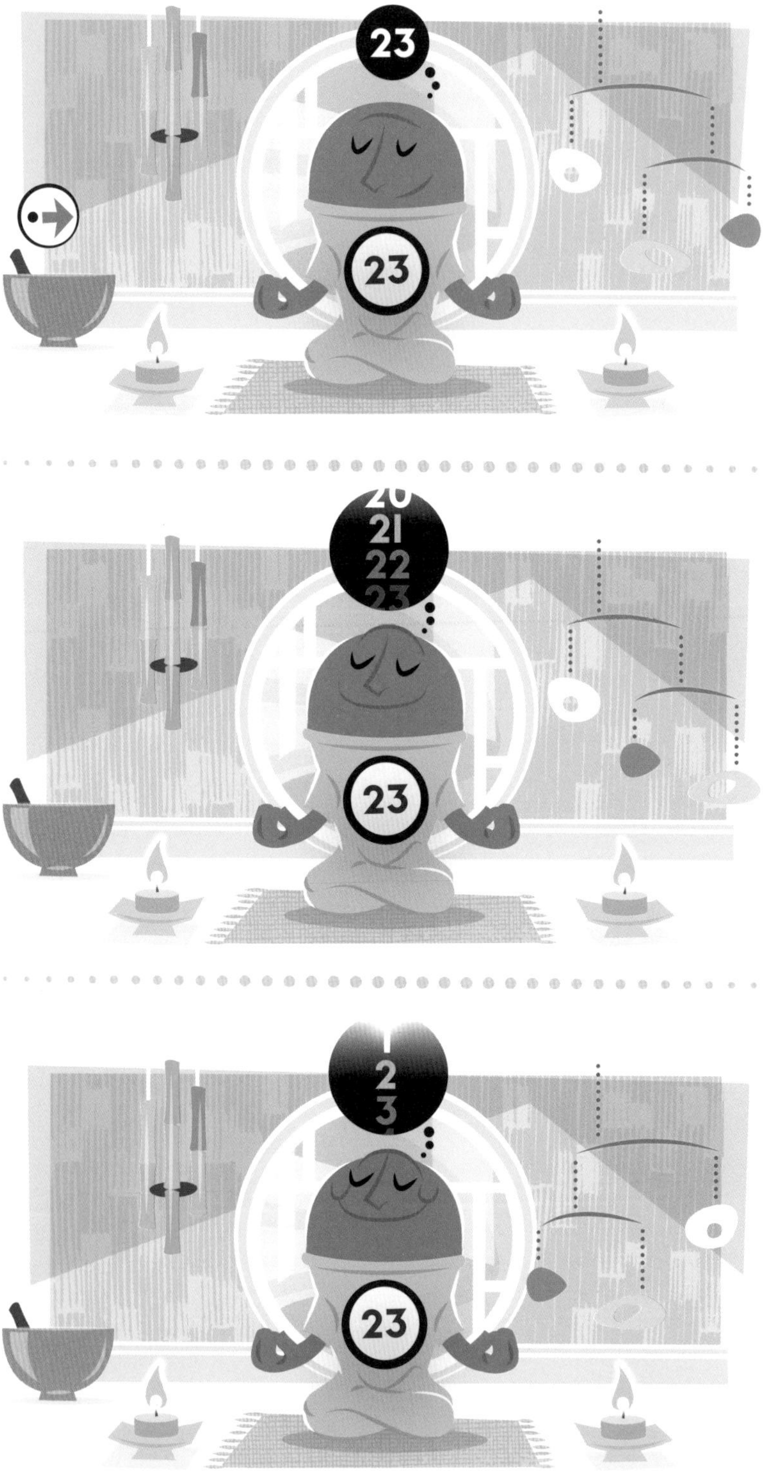
23
23
21
22
23
23
2
3
23

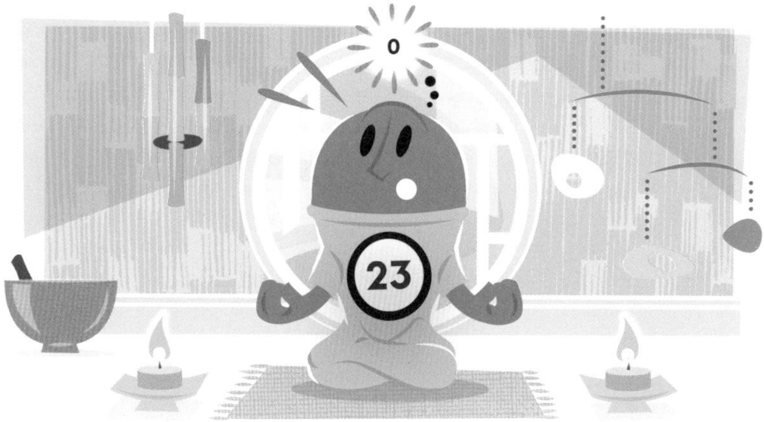
0
23

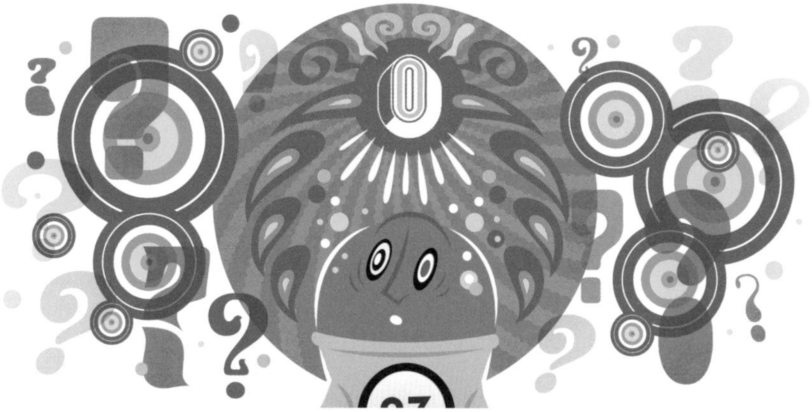

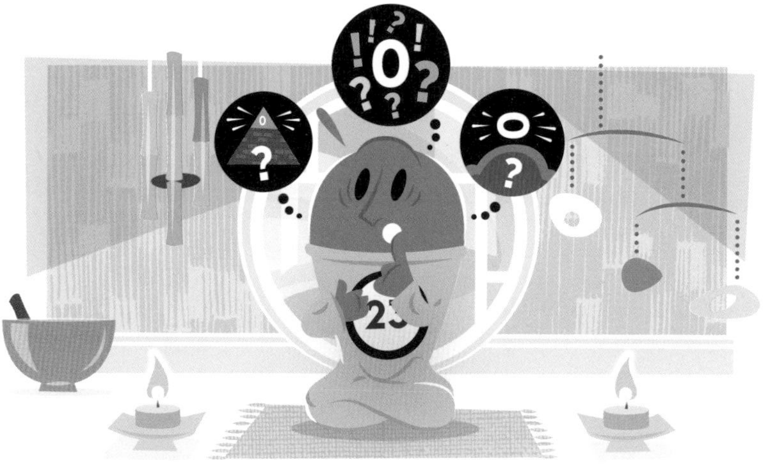
0

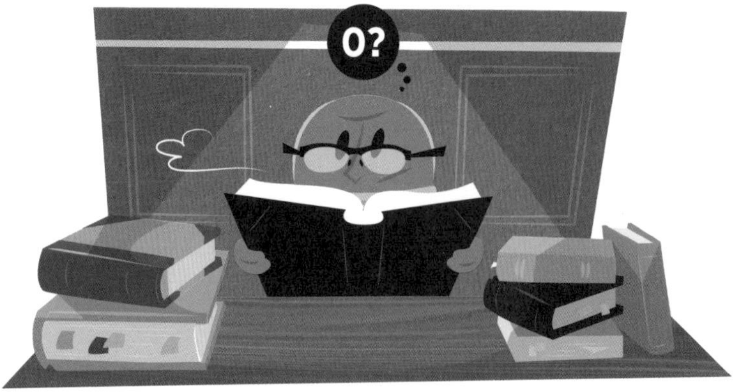
O?

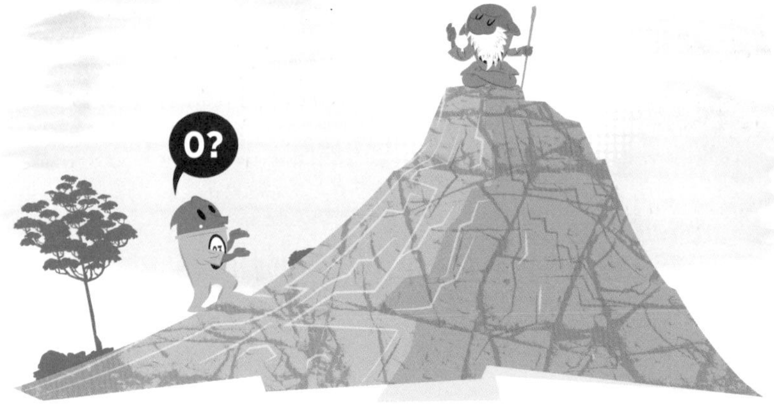
O?

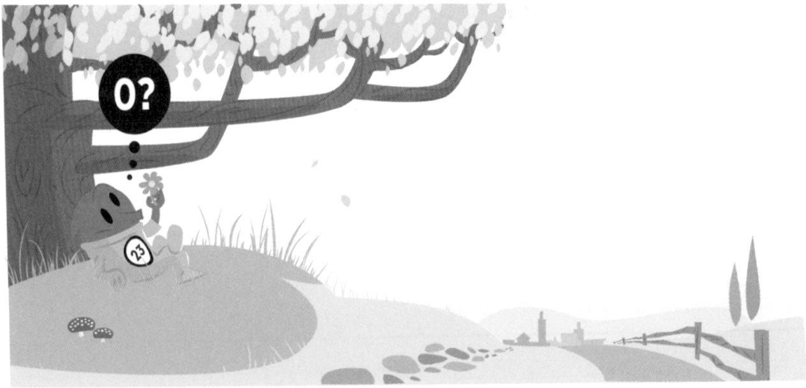
O?
23

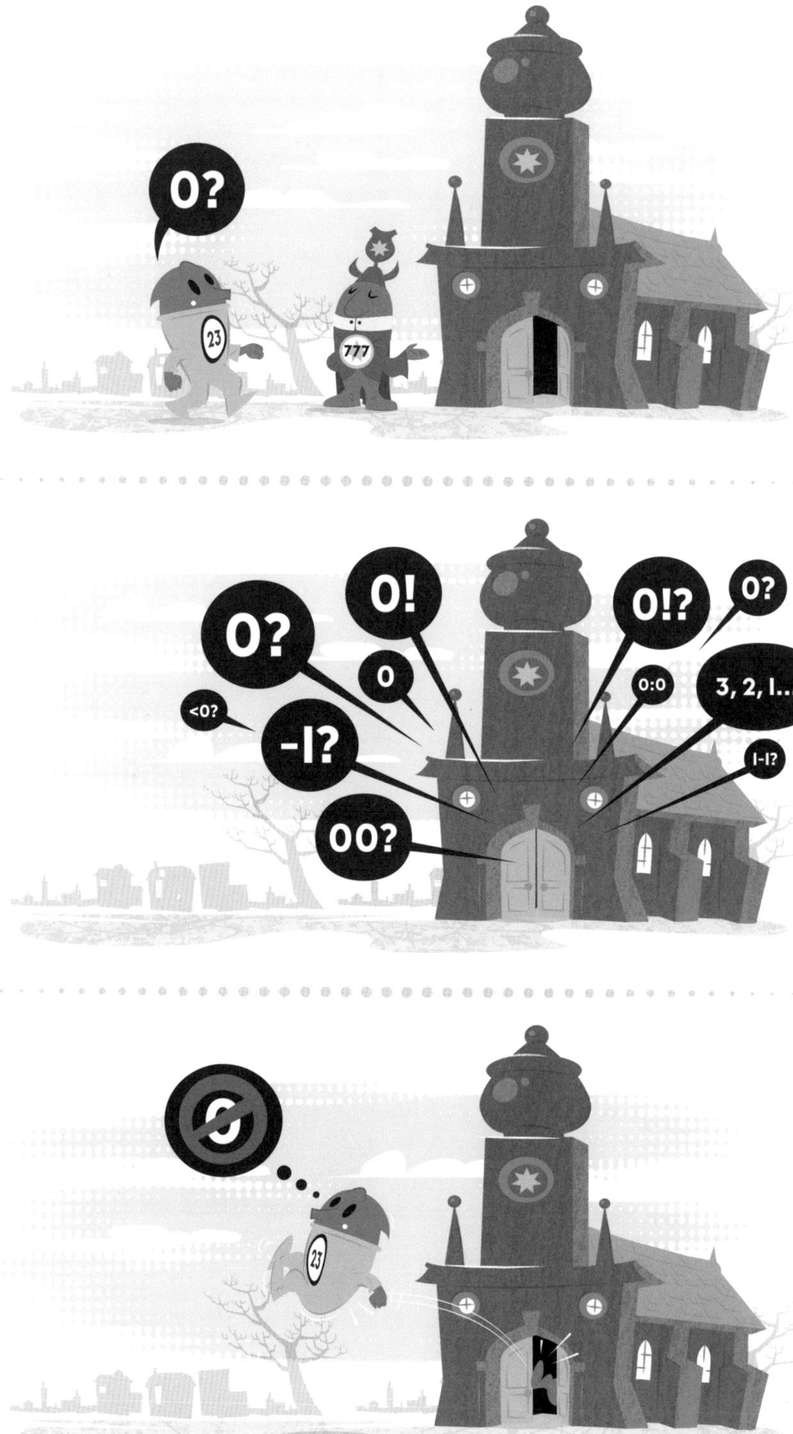
0?
0?
0!
0
<0?
-1?
00?
0!?
0?
0:0
3, 2, 1...?
1-1?

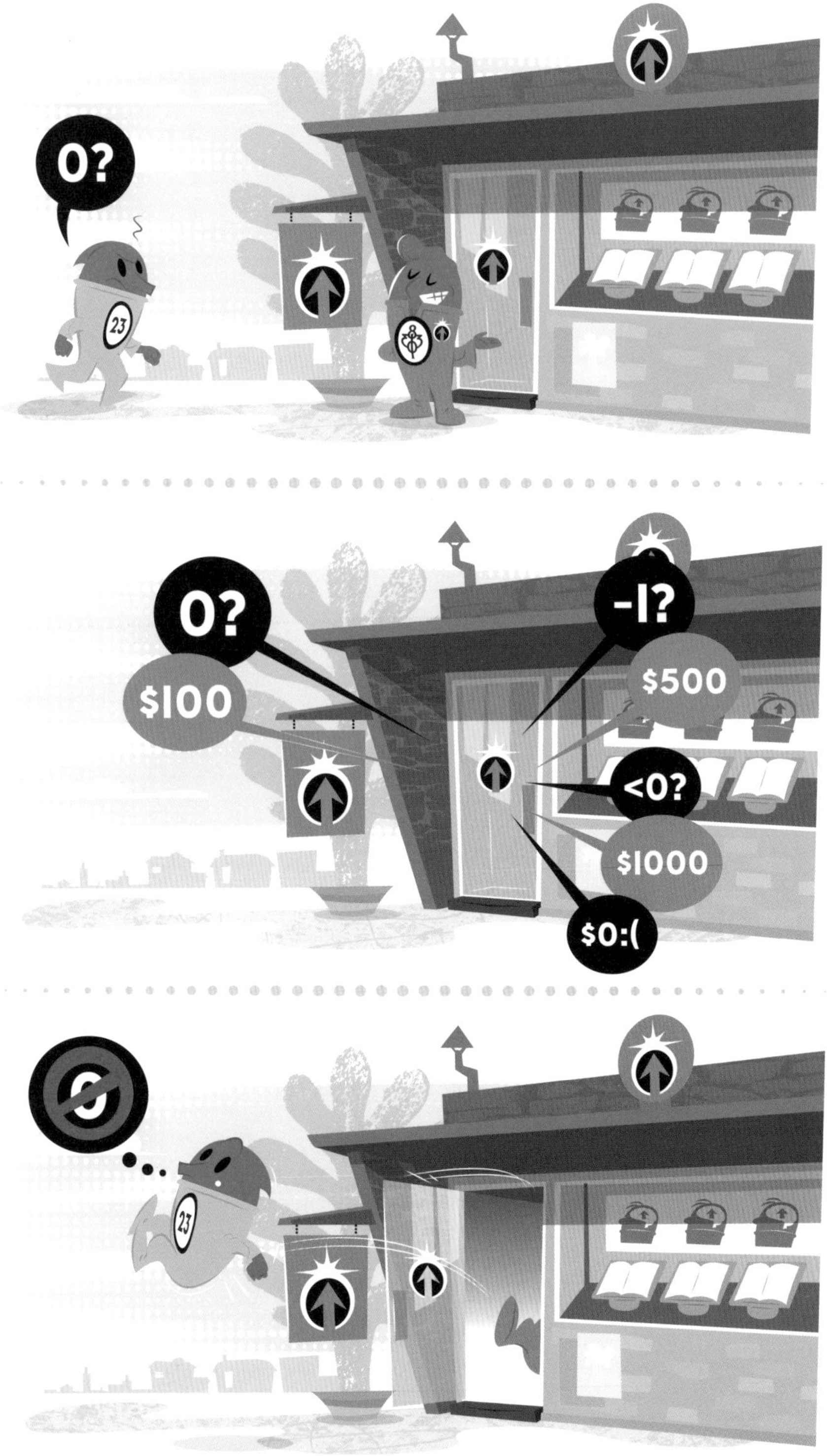
0?
23
0?
$100
-1?
$500
<0?
$1000
$0:(
23

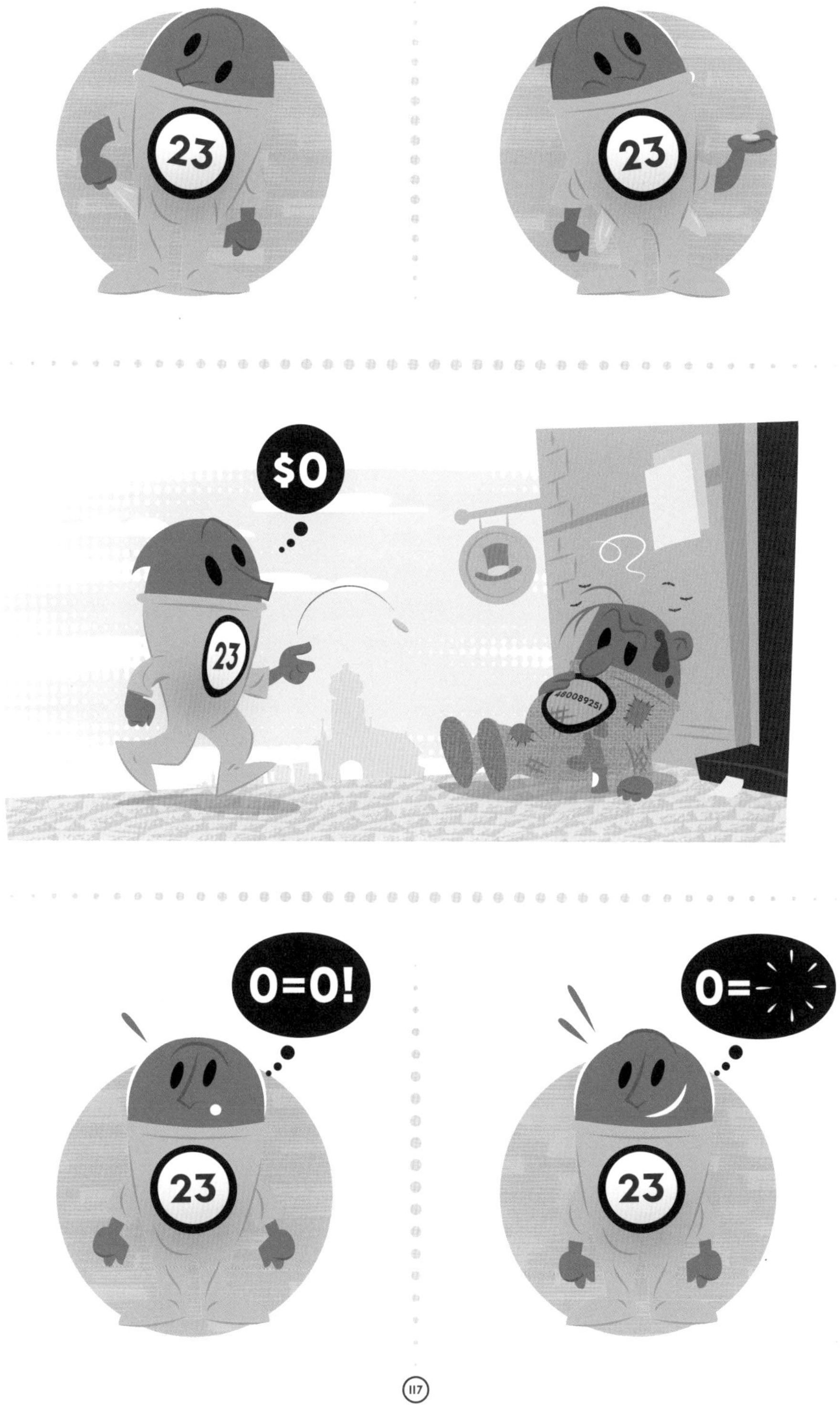
23
23
$0
23
480089251
0=0!
23
0=
23

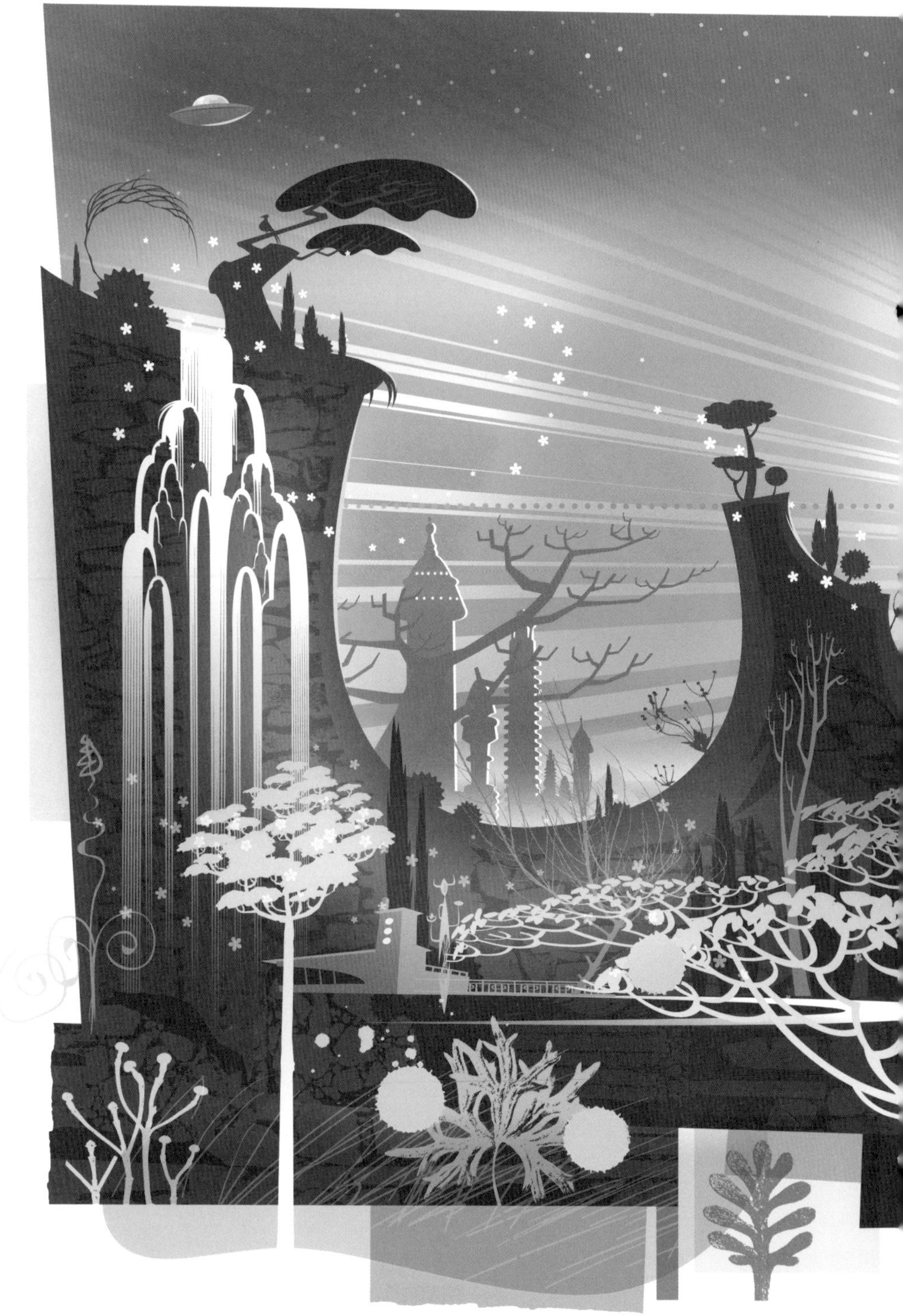

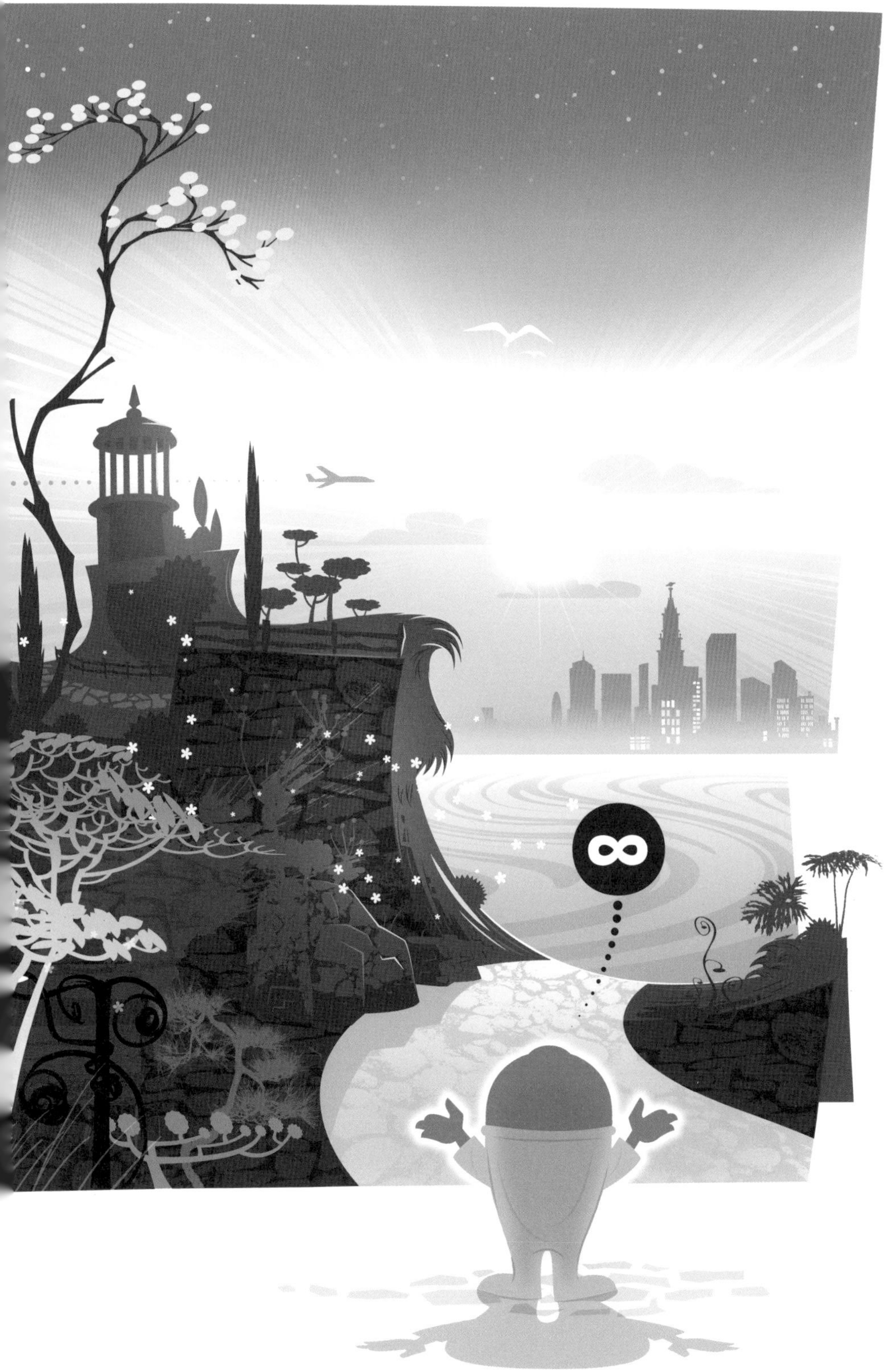

Rian Hughes is a graphic designer, illustrator, comic artist, author and typographer who has worked extensively for the British and American advertising, music and comic book industries.

He has produced CD and vinyl sleeves for mainstream acts and obscure indie labels, Hawaiian shirts, ranges for Swatch and hundreds of logos for properties such as *James Bond, The X-Men, Hed Kandi, The Avengers* and *Batman*. His editorial illustrations have appeared in magazines in the UK, US and Japan.

Recently he wrote and drew strips for DC Comics' *Batman: Black and White* and Vertigo's *Magenta,* and was reunited with Grant Morrison for two tales in *Heavy Metal* magazine. His comic strips have been collected in *Yesterday's Tomorrows* and *Tales from Beyond Science,* and his burlesque art in *Soho Dives, Soho Divas*.

His fonts are available via his own label, Device Fonts.

Other books by Rian Hughes
XX
Logo à Gogo
Custom Lettering of the '20s and '30s
Get Lettering
Get Mapmaking
Vertigo CMYK: Magenta
Batman: Black and White
Typodiscography
II2 Hours
Lifestyle Illustration of the '50s
Tales from Beyond Science *with Mark Millar, John Smith, Alan McKenzie*
Soho Dives, Soho Divas
Cult-ure: Ideas can be Dangerous
Custom Lettering of the '40s and '50s
On The Line *with Rick Wright*
Yesterday's Tomorrows *with Raymond Chandler, Grant Morrison, John Freeman, Tom DeHaven*
Lifestyle Illustration of the '60s
Custom Lettering of the '60s and '70s
Ugenia Lavender *with Geri Halliwell*
Ten Year Itch
Art, Commercial
Dare *with Grant Morrison*
The Science Service *with John Freeman*